NATIONAL
FREEMASONS
LEAGUE

Dawn Dugan

Dedication

I always deeply admired Jacqueline Kennedy, and I suspect the seed was planted to love her family based on the common link between her family and mine. I always admired her quote that went something like this: "If you fail at raising your family, not much else you do matters." I always reminded myself of that while raising my kids, and I thank God for them. I dedicate this book to my three children. I love you. I am so very proud of the 3 of you. You have steel spines and hearts of gold, and I am so glad God made me your mother. Remember, never go in the tank.

Acknowledgment

To every first responder—police officers, firefighters, EMTs—who have ever laid their life, their mind, or their sanity on the line for strangers. To those who answer the call no matter the hour, who witness tragedy firsthand, who carry the burdens most of society will never understand. You are the backbone of decency in a world that increasingly rewards vanity over virtue.

But this is also a warning: you cannot be both a supporter of first responders and a fan of the NFL. The two are incompatible. The NFL—saturated with Freemasonic influence—has used, exploited, and discarded more first responders than any other American entity. It has created a culture that glorifies power, suppresses truth, and manufactures chaos that you, our protectors, are then left to clean up.

Supporting the NFL while claiming to back the blue, the firehouse, or the ambulance is hypocrisy. You cannot cheer for those who destabilize society and also pretend to stand with those who risk everything to hold it together. This nation needs to wake up and make a choice. I have made mine.

This book is also for the good men and women in uniform who have bravely served our country only to be silenced, discarded, or broken in the shadows by a system that doesn't want you to speak. May your stories be told. May the truth ring louder than the stadiums. May we all grab our stones, and in unison fire them at Goliath. We take our country back by diagnosing their evil for what it is, and eradicating it from society.

About the Author

The National Freemasons League is Dawn's debut book, written after spending 27 years with a man who transformed before her eyes. Her ex-husband, an NFL Freemason, suffers from a diagnosed Traumatic Brain Injury and Chronic Traumatic Encephalopathy due to his football career. This devastation destroyed their marriage and life together. Dawn experienced the dark underbelly of a secret society that she believes has allowed evil to flourish in America since its inception. From domestic abuse to targeted harassment, chemical manipulation, and surveillance, she endured what many cannot fathom. And yet, she lives to tell the truth, not just for herself—but for every woman, child, and innocent person who has suffered in silence. Dawn firmly believes it is time to expose freemasonry and eradicate it from our country.

Her book is both a warning and a call to action: to expose the hidden systems of power that operate unchecked, to stand up against Freemasonry and similar structures, and to reclaim our spiritual and moral compass. Dawn encourages readers to give Sundays back to God, to walk away from organizations like the NFL that thrive on invisible hierarchies and oppression, and to build a society rooted in God and family first, justice, truth, service, and love.

Table of Contents

Chapter 01
From Where It Began

Some stories are so twisted, so deeply embedded in shadows, that telling them almost feels like pulling secrets from under a rock. Most people wouldn't believe that these things happen in the real world. They sound like something out of a conspiracy theory or a dark thriller novel. But when it happens to you, when the pieces of your life crumble in front of your eyes, you start to understand just how much power is hidden beneath the surface. *And that's where my story begins—in the hidden, shadowy depths of the unimaginable.*

On September 27, 2022, my three children went to school and never came home, on my daughter's birthday, no less. Why am I suffering the worst imaginable horror other than death or kidnapping that a mother can feel? Why am I, a loving mother, subjected to this unfathomable pain? Even if your child is sick, you can still love and nurture them. You have each other for the big and the small, the mundane or the extraordinary. But why don't I have my kids? Where did they go? Why was this fate chosen for me? Simple. The NFL and Freemasonry.

My grandfather was a 33-degree freemason, and unbeknownst to me, he had promised me to the National Football League to help defeat what President Donald Trump calls the Cabal, or the Deep State. Can you imagine being offered up like a piece of property for some secret cause? I was human-trafficked to the most image-based business in

1

America—the National Football League, which owns its very own day of the week. My life has always been hard, but it became a nightmare in June 2013 when I was knocked backward by a former NFL offensive lineman lunged on top of me —-his massive body crushing his own unborn son inside of me, and choked me while six months pregnant. His massive hands wrapped around my neck crushing my windpipe and making my eyes feel like they were going to come out of my head. A moment that would forever alter my life and the life of my unborn child.

The odd thing is that I had spent many years watching him do pass protection, where he blasts his hands into a defensive lineman's chest. I had seen it countless times on the field, and I had always wondered what that felt like. Then one day, I found out—while carrying his own son. The very man who should have protected us instead became my worst nightmare.

What do two arms of an NFL offensive lineman feel like blasting into the chest of a woman carrying a six-month fetus? It felt like two sledgehammers simultaneously hitting my chest, the force carrying me off my feet and onto my master bed. There, he lunged on top of me and choked me and his own unborn son within an inch of our lives. Imagine fighting for breath, fighting for two lives, your own and that of your baby.

How did I get to that warm June day in 2013? How did I find myself married to a well-presenting psychopath? How did I become a victim of this web of lies and betrayal? It started on my pre-determined birth date of July 17, 1976. 7/17/1976—a date with significance far beyond what I could have imagined. It was to signify a revolution, according to what has been relayed to me. My grandfather, the 33-degree freemason, harnessed his connections in medicine to ensure that I would have a birthday to remember, as well as a Social Security card with equal numerical power. Freemasons love to use numbers.

These numbers held a power I was unaware of. My social security number starts with 333, signifying that I was the offspring of a 33-degree freemason. It would be given to me, unbeknownst to me, signaling to anyone I supplied the number to, whose granddaughter I was, and ensuring that one group was properly documenting me, while another group was misdocumenting me. Why both? Why this double life, this web of deceit? Because being born with 132 degrees of Freemasonry, I was four times as powerful as my grandfather. Therefore, he wanted to ensure I had built-in flaws. I was both a treasure and a threat. My personality was created based on his research with top psychiatrists, I am told. A manufactured identity created in a lab, not from love but for an agenda.

How do you create a strong child? Give them poverty. As a child, I was always perplexed why my dad, who was so smart, could not get a job. He was not a drug addict. He drank, but I never remember seeing him fall down drunk. I did, however, recall seeing grown-ups start trouble with him most times he was in public. The constant struggle of a man who was kept down by forces beyond his control.

One day, the truth was told to me by three friends, all strangers to one another, yet each telling the same stories of what they were witnessing in masonic meetings. Three different people, same story—the pieces began to fall into place. It all made sense. My dad was being gang-stalked or directly targeted.

The elite billionaires were using the government to attack one of their own citizens just because he had more degrees than they did. A target, just as I had been. It is a term that, if you Google it, you will see is used on many people worldwide. Why is it worldwide? Simple—the Freemasons are worldwide. Their power knows no boundaries. My goal in writing this book? It is to wrap freemasonry in dynamite, globally, and blow it to smithereens. My goal is to destroy Freemasonry as if they were my most hated sports opponent. I will not fail, for I know God is on my side, as well as millions of decent human beings, globally, who are ready to expose this wicked, evil, useless form of invisible slavery. Now that I have told you my goal in writing this book, let me tell you more about me.

From the day I was born, based on information disseminated to me by these three friends who witnessed the NFL masonic meetings, much of my life was predetermined. Predetermined, yet unknown to me—my life controlled from the shadows. As was my dad's. My dad is a mechanical genius. He can take apart anything engine-wise or mechanical and put it back together by memory. A brilliant mind held hostage by a system that refused to let him succeed. I found a stack of inventions that he sent to Washington, D.C. None were ever accepted because he was not allowed to be rich or make money. However, my hunch is that someone got rich off his ideas and outside-the-box creative genius. But it wasn't him.

It just wasn't him.

Chapter 02

Grandma

My paternal grandmother was my north star. She would garden and cook meals from scratch. She loved Pyrex glass dishes and cast-iron skillets. I can remember her boiling vegetables or making her own chicken and dumplings from scratch. I would later learn from a friend who witnessed the masonic meetings that my 33-degree grandpa loved her Chicken and Dumplings and called her Dumplin'. Cannot prove it, but I believe it was based on how good her Chicken and Dumplings were. She had brand loyalty to certain brands that she passed along to me. I now have come to see that as more than buying the best this or that —but more about aligning myself with the help that was supposed to come one day. From what I understand, many of those brands have shown up for me in masonic meetings, and I thank them for that. When you show up for me, you show up for all of humanity.

Grandma and her cousin Helen Voges met 2 men, best friends, who were out for a night on the town at a dance hall called Casa Loma Ballroom, in St. Louis, Missouri. The 2 best friends were named Harlan "Buddy" Gurney and Charles Augustus Lindbergh, the famed aviator. Their meeting, however, was before Lindbergh's famed trip across the Atlantic Ocean that would make him an international superstar. He and Gurney were just airmail pilots running mail around the Midwest in small airplanes for Robertson Aircraft, based out of Lambert Field.

My grandmother was an honest, direct, no-nonsense woman. She was loyal. She wrote everything down. I credit her with my ability to document. She wrote down the most mundane details so beautifully, not realizing that many times, we can see anomalies in the mundane that we can see patterns. I still have many things she documented. I believe that she learned this penchant for documenting from Lindbergh. We lived in a trailer not far from her little white house that set off the road. One of my most vivid memories, besides her escorting us to the zoo, complete with a picnic lunch she made, is I remember her light in her bedroom, which sat at the back of her house. The light would commonly turn on in the middle of the night. If one walked up to her window, one would find her sitting with her feet on the floor, but positioned sitting with her feet off the side of her bed. Grandma would worry and worry and worry. Her home had long been paid off. I often wondered what kept her up at night with seemingly no enormous mortgage to pay, and then, in the past few years, I have come to know what kept her up at night. I suspect she was worried that she knew I was headed for a life of hardship. She knew I would one day be human trafficked to a man who would destroy my life in the name of freedom.

My grandma was so good to me. I remember arguing with my dad one day. I was upset that we were so poor and that our house was so chaotic. Her house was a refuge for me. One day, I ran to her house crying and went into the closet in the room I would sleep in while with her, and the door locked behind me. I banged on the closet door, crying until Grandma rescued me. She was a godly woman who baptized me at a Lutheran Church in Columbia, IL. Imagine how I feel in the place where she baptized me before God— that one day the pastor who baptized me would one day vote against me in masonic meetings, therefore vote for my continued suffering, vote for my kids to continue to be endangered. The NFL is a powerful seductress. It is like a moth to flame for people with low self-esteem. They used the oldest psychology techniques to make you feel like you are left out if you aren't in the know about what is happening in the NFL. That is the Power of the Good Ole Boys Club. To them, a brain-injured psychopathic NFL player is better than a traumatized, reactive, abuse woman. I don't ever see that changing. Disband the pyramid of Racketeering, and they still try to run it their way, with their rules, with their MEN in charge. (No, I am not talking about Donald Trump. Trump actually had the nerve to speak publicly about the brain injuries the NFL is causing.)

My grandma would read the bible. She had baby blue leather luggage that I was told was bought by Lindbergh, as well as the paid-off house. I cannot prove it, but it certainly makes sense. I remember when Grandma got the call that Geraldine had passed away. She cried and was so upset. Geraldine was the daughter of her cousin Helen Voges and Buddy Gurney. Sadly, Helen died at the age of 33 in 1940.

After Helen died, Buddy had small children and no wife. He would go on to marry Grandma's other cousin, Hilda Voges, Helen's little sister. They would raise Helen and Buddy's children and add their own daughter, named Hilda, after her mother, to the family. I spoke with Hilda (Jr) not long ago and really enjoyed talking to her. She reminds me of my grandma.

Direct, no-nonsense. Hilda confirmed to me our family history of the incidence of colon cancer that runs in the family. After Helen died in July 1940, Grandma would become pregnant not long after with my dad. A man named Lee Dugan from southern Missouri would step in and marry my grandma when she was around 6 months pregnant. I never knew Grandpa Dugan. He died in 1957 when my dad was a teenager. My dad loved him. He spoke very highly of him, and I imagine he was a high-level Freemason that Lindbergh moved into the role of father for my dad, who was born August 15, 1941. There are many heroes in this story, and Lee Dugan is one of them. He lost his first wife, and I hope to learn more about her family as I research family history.

I suspect that unbeknownst, the Voges sisters, as well as Grandma, were guided to certain men because Grandma's family came from a very well-respected German family named the Arras Family. The Arras family had been given a castle by Otto the Great, the German ruler, for the 12 strong Arras sons to help defeat the Huns when the Huns were trying to invade Southern Germany. The Castle, along with the hidden masonic lineage, now resides in Alf, Germany. The beautiful castle that the leader of Germany bestowed upon my ancestors is called Burg Arras Castle. It is breathtaking, with amazing views in all directions. I was able to visit the castle in 2000. It was more beautiful than I could have imagined. My Grandma and her cousins were carrying 33 degrees, so her getting pregnant with Lindbergh's child meant a 66 degree dad. That single sentence that I just typed finally explained a lifetime of questions and puzzling experiences.

The day in 1982 when Geraldine, the daughter of Buddy and Helen died was so hard for Grandma. I now understand why, now that I am a parent. Geraldine was likely like a daughter to Grandma, so it was like Grandma had lost her own child. My grandma called my dad "Buddy" his entire life. An ode to Buddy Gurney, I suppose. I don't think that it is a coincidence that my parents were married on April 9th, in the late 1960s. That particular date in April happened to be the same day that Lindbergh and Gurney took their very first flight together on April 9, 1922 with pilot Otto Timm. The flight took place in Omaha, Nebraska at the Nebraska Aircraft Corporation Flying School. I don't recall ever meeting Buddy or Hilda Sr., but I do recall answering the phone a lot at Grandma's house and getting the family that I now know called from out west. Gurney had moved his family from St. Louis to California.

I did not know I was the granddaughter of Charles Lindbergh until a visit to the Missouri History Museum in St. Louis 2 years ago. I had been there many times with my kids but on this visit my kids had been stolen by their dad for 3 months. I was so lonely and to counter missing my 3 best friends, I went to the History Museum. That day at the Missouri History Museum I took my time. The upper floor had a Charles Lindbergh exhibit and I came face to face with a photo that felt like my father was staring back at me. A few days later my co-worker, Anita Arnold, at Harwell Media Group in O'Fallon, asked me if I felt like I was related to Charles Lindbergh. I had not mentioned his name so I immediately felt like this information was being disclosed to me for a purpose. I had filed for a divorce from an NFL player and must have done about 100 one-click applications on a job site. The only one of two jobs I could secure an interview for was with Reginald and Stephanie Harwell, 2 retired Air Force Veterans who both finished in the top 1 percent of the military.

I want to be clear on something. I don't feel like I need a royal title or validation of who I am. I am someone with nothing attached to me because I fear and worship God and am a good person. The more I read about Lindbergh, the more I love him. I think he wanted to destroy Freemasonry. He wanted people to be seen as equals. He was simplistic. There was a photo my grandma had that had her in a dress and a grey-haired man in a white shirt and blue suit pants. It said on the back, Charles and I. When I googled Lindbergh, I saw the same man in the same outfit in a Google photo. If I can speak for him, I think he wants these things; He wants Freemasonry exposed. He wants people to be kind. To help the homeless, the disabled, and the poor. He wants us to break our addiction to things that harm our bodies, brains, and family units, as well as what harms the planet. He wants us to work hard and live within our means. to do more gardening, more crocheting. He wants us to tell the truth, so we don't have to remember a lie. He wants children around the planet to have safe and protected childhoods. I believe that he was the biggest influence on my grandma and shaped her forward-thinking on holistic medicine.

I also feel the need to defend Charles Lindbergh from attacks. He was viewed negatively for not keeping in touch with people. He had a genius mind going 100 miles per minute, and he was a problem solver. He was always finding problems and doing what he could to solve them, as evidenced by his inventing the perfusion pump, alongside Dr. Alexis Carrel. He was simply a busy man trying to solve as many problems as possible. One of them is to make the world a better place, and unbeknownst to many, crafting a plan to free the world from the invisible form of slavery called freemasonry. Also, many have tried to paint Lindbergh as a nazi. That is 100 percent false. Here is how I view it. Lindbergh was a decent, honest man. He was the leader of the good team on the Freemason board. He had a 95 percent approval rating with the American Public. Had he decided to run for president, evil would have been unemployed and homeless. The evil, greedy Freemasons set him up. evil freemasons in government sent him on a goodwill visit to Nazi Germany under the guise that he was taking note of what type of planes and weapons that they have. They used those photos of him visiting Nazi Germany to tarnish him in the public eye. He was 100 percent right to be leery of entering the war until all the facts were known. He also was aware of the Military Industrial Complex that tended to drive the US towards war strictly to enrich the companies that they owned that supplied the US Government with items needed to facilitate a war. Let me be 100 percent clear. Every single soldier who has died for America, has died for a noble cause. They either died for legitimate purposes of war, or to expose that there were elite freemasons leading us to war to launder taxpayer dollars to their own companies or to companies of their cronies.

I found solace at my grandma's. It was organized, clean, and orderly, with no loud TV blaring. My dad worked on generators in the Army and was left with hearing loss. It would cause him to blare the TV at def con in our trailer. His mind was always thinking. He had the TV always blaring and I blame that TV always being on for part of my sleep patterns. However, my grandma's house was always very quiet and calm. My grandma had just a small black and white TV that she would watch often. She loved The Waltons and Little House on The Prairie. Next to the TV were plants like Aloe Vera. She also would put up a small Christmas tree each Christmas. Her kitchen looked out into the backyard, and her flowers she would tend to.

One of my favorite memories is of dying Easter Eggs with my grandma. She would then hide them in her tulip garden for me and my brother to find. She was loving and kind. I can hear her say my name, "Little Dawn-eee." I lost her in college when I was still just a dumb, young kid. I never thought of the important questions I wished I could have asked her until way later.

She kept a stack of birthday cards and personal cards that she received at the top of her closet. I enjoyed getting them down and reading them. My grandma was no frills. What mattered to her was family. She wore the same few dresses over and over. She would make me quilts, including the one with 34 degrees hidden in the quilt. That quilt is the silent testament to me that this story is true. I was created to be made 34 degrees. I was created to expose and destroy freemasonry. Grandma never talked about it, though. She just raised me with her ideals and attitude, knowing that one day I would understand the meaning hidden in the quilt. I can understand why she sat on that bed worrying. She had good reason to worry. Other than death, I imagine I am living pretty close to what can be considered tragic. I have 3 beautiful children that I birthed and raised, only to have them ripped from my life while having a gang of people attempt to frame a woman whose life was destroyed as a bad person instead of a traumatized, and reactive-abuse person. I went to a church knowing who does and doesn't vote for me in Masonic meetings. It is beyond cruel and inhumane, and the majority of my pain isn't inflicted only by the Satanists but also by the Christians. I am waiting for God to show me why. Why have your disciples who recited bible verses shown no compassion or empathy —or, more importantly, urgency in getting my kids home?

This Truman Show (my friend Nathan told me that I am watched like the main character in The Truman Show) of my life has shown what greed can do to society. Hopefully, it shows how well a psychopath presents. CTE has become a buzzword in recent years, and for good reasons. It stands for Chronic Traumatic Encephalopathy. It is a degenerative disease, meaning it gets worse each day that goes by. If it was given to you by the NFL? If you are their player or former player, you are going to get a team of people to help frame the abused woman while you get reports making you look like Einstein while covering up that you were the worst brain out of 300. Anything bad that you have done will be covered up. And it isn't much since, in high school, you got the playbook for winning The Chosen One as well as the manual for destroying the real Chosen One.

The NFL runs on false idol worship, brain damage, abuse, control, and corruption. People, some unknowingly, spend their paychecks to consume childhoods. That is how far the Satanists have infiltrated America. They get people to work jobs they sometimes hate for poor pay, for 40 hours per week, then get them to hand that hard-earned money over to the NFL to watch a man slowly brain injured, a marriage likely destroyed, and childhoods consumed.

As a child, I was very aware that we were poor. I hated it. I vowed to go to college and work hard, and ensure that I never lived like my parents had to live. Now I live worse based on the suffering of missing my 3 children. I also have much more debt than my parents ever had. I am 48 years old and living in their basement after being put into what my college friend and former ABC News Emmy award-winning journalist friend Mark Greenblatt described as The Destabilization Program, something he had only witnessed put onto people leaving The White House or The Pentagon. The Destabilization Program is what was done when that person needed to be discredited, so they were put into the

Destabilization Program, so no one would believe the story that they were about to tell. I imagine I am not the only NFL wife put into the government-backed program called The Destabilization Program to hide the greed-damaged brains that turned them into abusers. When I began to read up on the program, I would see it also called COINTELPRO. It is essentially the rich elite, using the government and therefore government employees to attack a citizen whom they don't like. The elite have been doing this, most likely, since the inception of our country.

Chapter 03
High School

In Junior High, I tried out for Cheerleading and did not make it to the team. I was as upset as any junior high girl would be. As a child, I had begun a basketball program that reminded me of my beloved Harlem Globetrotters. We would learn basic ball handling drills and then be brought out to Varsity Basketball games to perform. We would do the machine gun, also a figure eight dribbling drill, and spin the ball on our fingers. I loved it. I loved the music that would play as we performed. I can remember Rebel Rouser, Johnny B Goode, and more. That began my love of basketball, which continued through Junior High and High School and today. I grew up not far from downtown St. Louis. I grew up poor. I was not one of the most popular students in Junior High. Any popularity that I gained in High School contributed to being a good athlete.

I played volleyball, basketball, and softball all four years of high school. I was Junior and Senior Class President. Being a class officer earned me free tickets to The Muny, which is an outdoor, live theatre located in a park in St. Louis. The Muny made me experience the Arts in person in a way that I never had before. I loved it. I loved getting dressed up, seeing the actors perform, and hearing the orchestra music. I felt like that small thing, attending The Muny, allowed me to get a glimpse of how successful people are allowed to enjoy life. We were poor. Very poor. We lived paycheck to paycheck. If any money was in the checking account, then magically, the car broke down, and that was the amount that was due. I really could not imagine a life where there were days when I would find myself experiencing nice vacations. As a child, I dreamed of nice houses, nice vacations, and a family. That is what drove my work ethic, that, when traumatized, is not matched. I learned from a therapist that the key to surviving trauma is fantasy. I think I defaulted to dreaming big to survive the trauma of a poor childhood.

I worked hard in high school with the sole goal of outworking poverty. Odd how that works. I didn't know then about freemasonry and what it would do to my life after I had worked so hard. I am aware I am not the only one. There are thousands of us. They, too, have their story to tell if they wish. My dad was always firm on not trying drugs (He said they might kill you the first time), not getting tattoos, and being honest. I dated a guy in college with tattoos. I don't discount anyone with them; it was just ingrained in me not to get one, and I don't think I would like one, but as you can see, I dated a guy with a tattoo. Many people will hold it against me for saying that, but everyone's parents installed software into their child, even if they didn't realize it and even if they disagree with it. When you respect your dad, you do what he asks so that he will continue to treat you like a human. Psychiatry at work in how I was raised and I don't doubt it came from the brightest minds.

My dad was perpetually warning me about kidnappings. After learning I was Lindbergh's granddaughter, left with 132 degrees of lineage, I understood why my dad worried so much about me dying. We watched True Crime together, and I remember him warning me when there were happenings at a local mall where criminals were hiding under cars and then attacking women. I now see why my dad was so concerned with my welfare. He was aware that I was a prize in the invisible Game of Thrones. He had to ensure I made it to college, where I would be handed over to an NFL player to stack the NFL Masonic Team with The Chosen One. Not my words. These were just the words conveyed to me by three people, strangers to one another, but partners in witnessing the NFL Masonic Meetings.

As a child, my brother had mini-helmets of all the NFL teams. We would play with them. His favorite was Barry Sanders and the Detroit Lions. There are no coincidences. Lindbergh's close friend was Ford Motor Company owner Henry Ford. Therefore, the Lions were my favorite as a small child. I had no idea at the time, but I do now that Detroit was the birthplace of Lindbergh. Also, the owner of the NFL team in Detroit was a personal friend of his. My brother's favorite NFL team was instilled in him to instill in me so that one day, a future NFL player would find my love of football appealing and then deliver himself a one-way ticket to the NFL and me to my human traffickers to have my life destroyed while being framed out of my children.

My brother also loved Oklahoma Football. Therefore, I loved Oklahoma Football. They had a talented and brash linebacker in the early 1980s named Brian Bosworth. The Boz, as he was called, was flamboyant and opinionated. He attempted to take on the NCAA, the governing body of all college athletes. That, and his on the field performance, led him to nationwide notoriety. His book is one of my favorites. I remember reading how he talked about how people hate you, part of them hate themselves. People hate people who make them feel something without their consent. It made sense to me. I remind myself of his words when I think of hating someone for reasons other than them being evil people who are knowingly trying to cause harm to innocent kids, to me, or both of us. I am human, and from time to time, I have to tell myself to knock it off if I feel jealous of someone or hating on someone for reasons other than being evil. I remind myself that it reflects more on me than it does on them. It is important we see evil and deal with it in society.

I finished high school with 12 varsity letters and a determination to work hard in college and never be poor again. The summer before my senior year, I was invited by the daughter of a policeman to the batting cages. There, I would meet Matt Russell. He was working at the batting cages and, therefore, standing outside the batting cages when I came out. He asked me if I played softball at the University of Kentucky, probably because I was wearing one of their sweatshirts. No, I told him I don't play there. I told him that I was still in high school. I told him that he looked like The Boz, and I think that must have impressed him because he told me he played Linebacker for the University of Colorado and that he was home for the summer. I was so dumb back then. I thought it was fate. I had no idea that I was being introduced to one of my NFL arranged marriage options. It did not matter.

I was definitely smitten with Matt. I would later figure out that Matt is a renegade, free thinker. He was guided away from me because the NFL masonic handler put into place to ensure my future NFL player husband was going to agree to destroy my life, and I can tell you right now, based on the way Matt is, he was never going to do that. He would not willingly agree to do that. They didn't tell him the truth about why the masons were guiding him away from me, but they succeeded. I am aware of why Matt fled from my life based on my looks. I still agree that he was raised better than to do to me what they were going to require of him. Craig, though, I know would and did agree to destroy my life. I never saw it coming.

I wanted to graduate and get a great job, a nice house, and have a family. That's all. I wanted the American Dream, but later, I would learn that I was getting the opposite. I was getting The American Nightmare that would turn the most image-based business in the country, the NFL, into an entity that wanted to destroy my life simply because their sport destroyed my husband's brain. Think about that. The NFL owners have known since the 1950s that players were turning punch drunk. Their brains resembled those of professional boxers who would come down with a syndrome that made them act irrationally, sometimes harming others or losing all their money, or worse. The brain damage that manifests in football players is degenerative, meaning it gets worse every day. Researchers have stated that the worst behavior shows up 10 years after the final hits. I believe that to be true. Craig Heimburger took his final NFL snap in 2003, and was knocking me backward and choking me 6 months pregnant in 2013.

I was offered one scholarship in high school for softball. I remember having interest shown in me for basketball from Illinois College. My thinking was that I needed to choose the sport that I was best at, and I felt like that was softball. I had inquired if the University of Illinois had a softball team and was told no, that they didn't. I visited the campus of the University of Missouri in Columbia. There, I had an epiphany during the visit that that is where I wanted to be. I felt like God was guiding me there.

I had grown up watching Mizzou athletics on TV and decided that I would pursue walking on to their softball team. I contacted the Mizzou Head Coach, Jay Miller, to tell him of my interest in walking on. Then I drove down for a visit with my brother. He was wearing an Oklahoma starter jacket, and I didn't think about that at the time, but how it must have looked to have a walk-on's brother bringing her to visit Mizzou in one of their arch-rivals' fan gear. Mizzou's Coach told me that I could walk on and then earn a scholarship after a year. I was pleased with that news. I did not have a college fund. I had parents who lived in a trailer and were barely getting by. As a child, I had to walk next door in the freezing cold in order to take a hot bath in the 1990s.

A few weeks after graduating from high school in 1994, an NFL player was in the news for being a suspect in the murder of his ex-wife and her friend. I had no idea that one day, I would see that case in a completely different manner. That one day, I would look back on it as a PowerPoint presentation for CTE and freemasonry, as well as greed.

Nicole Brown Simpson was a stunning 36-year-old when she was bludgeoned to death and nearly decapitated in June 1994 in Brentwood, California. Her ex-husband, former NFL player Orenthal James Simpson, penned a suicide note and fled from the police. I looked at it then as just another crime. Now I look at it for what it is. NFL Freemasons, greed, and CTE. OJ was knowingly having his brain stolen from him, one hit at a time. The Frontal lobes govern logic, reasoning, impulse control, and the ability to predict the consequences of one's choices. I believe that the suspected killer, Former NFL player O.J. Simpson, had what Dr. Daniel Kelly would explain as a "walking brain injury." I will go into more detail on that later.

Nicole would tell her sisters, "he is going to kill me, and he is going to get away with it." The police would be called several times over OJ's beating of Nicole, but the police seemed powerless to help her. I didn't know it then, but I know now that the police were powerless because of the invisible pyramid scheme that runs our country called Freemasonry. The NFL elite billionaires use their money, power, and masonic degrees to run our government with their power and influence. I can see the NFL freemasonry at work in the stories of when the police were leaking information about who were the star witnesses.

That was not a cognizant decision of a "dirty cop." That was the orders from the elite NFL Freemasons telling the police to help end this PR nightmare of their cash cow that supplied them with endless riches, including lavish mansions, luxury cars, vacation homes, and a staff of servants. Nicole Brown

Simpson was a nobody to the NFL owners. Her death was merely a threat to their cash cow. They wanted anyone but O.J. Simpson to be found responsible, and they did their darndest to ensure that he was found innocent, and it worked. The NFL Freemasons' ability to control the police was going to ensure that their player was not found guilty of a grotesque crime that the majority of the population today would openly admit that they think he committed.

I see the O.J. Simpson case as much more than that. I see the NFL's masonic greed and control of the police, which my ex-NFL player husband explained to me. I see the character assassination of the victims by the power brokers of the pyramid scheme, and I can relate. I feel intense hurt for Nicole, knowing she knew what I knew but could not quite explain. She had no way of knowing that the NFL owners knew that OJ was punch drunk. They knew he had a walking brain injury, and that he would one day unleash it on her and that she would die. That is business negligence if you or I do it. If the NFL does it? It is another day at the office. The NFL runs off hiding walking brain injuries, character assassinating victims, then using teachers and coaches to brainwash the children that no dad didn't kill mom. No NFL player with battered logic, reasoning, and impulse control parts of the brain would do that to the woman he was terrorizing, due to his employer running the police. Right? Wrong.

It is unconscionable and reprehensible what the Simpson kids have been put through and what my kids have been put through, and what a countless number of other kids have been put through. Telling this story is an attempt to make sure it never happens again. I sit here while it has been two years without my children in my daily life, with hints of someone making my life right, while nothing happens. No one is making it right at all. They are all worried about money and not stolen childhoods. Meanwhile, their children are pampered and given extravagant lifestyles, while my children live with a man with broken frontal lobes, the logic, reasoning, and impulse control center of the brain.

Chapter 04
What Led from the College

I arrived at the University of Missouri-Columbia in August 1994, wearing a cross necklace that signified my belief in Jesus. To prepare for tryouts, which my coach insisted I complete to make the team, I bought Wheaties and Raisin Bran. At a team BBQ, I met a teammate with whom I connected well. We attended church together and discussed our faith in God. Just before our friendship ended following my divorce from an NFL player, she referred to me as "The Chosen One." I understood what she meant; she was alluding to the idea that I would stop freemasonry and become well-known due to my grandfather, who was a 33-degree lifetime Freemason. Interestingly, she is married to a man whose mother has worked with the police for decades, and she had insider knowledge about my grandfather and my own experience with human trafficking in the National Football League.

Returning to the fall of 1994, I successfully made the Mizzou Softball Team. As a child, while playing sports with my brother and his friends, if I cried, I was quickly pulled aside and admonished for it. It was ingrained in me from a young age: no crying. I believe the reason I was pushed into sports early on and taught this mantra of "no crying" was to toughen me up for what lay ahead. My grandfather likely aimed to mentally prepare me for an uncertain future, which involved being human trafficked to the NFL.

Today, I find myself living a nightmare sponsored by the National Football League. I've been told that if I do or do not do certain things, or if I stop discussing the brain injury that has disrupted both my husband's life and my own, including my ability to swallow food properly, my life will improve. I've been waiting for two years. I was seen as a means to produce 33-degree Masonic offspring, only to be discarded like NFL wife trash once they were finished with me. I'm not alone in this; there are several others, if not dozens, who share this experience.

It is hard for me to fathom. I know millions that are viewing this in the Masonic meeting, and that many care. Many are envious, and they think living their life earned them the right to a hidden prestige or something that I have. I am not sure. All I know is that fame and money bring out the worst in people. I met a woman who has happy kids, an adoring husband, and a nice home. She is allowed to work a job and earn more money than minimum wage, but she didn't like that I was getting votes when she did so much more for the church. I have literally had my children ripped from my life—-everything that she takes for granted —-and yet how I don't help as much as she does at church is the dealbreaker.

I will say this, Lindbergh and the doctors and psychiatrists he consulted with before giving me my childhood were spot on. So much of my childhood was about suffering. Suffering through poverty. Suffering through sports training. Suffering through so many things that when it came time for suffering CTE, and suffering the theft of my children by the NFL freemasons, I felt prepared. Whoever advised him did a great job, because I am in a place mentally that they will never beat me, because I will never quit. I will rest. But I will do many other things to cope with the horrific pain of missing my children each day, but I will never quit. I encourage you to rest but don't quit if you are in a similar situation to mine. God hears your prayers. Please pray often like I do.

I have fond memories of my college softball days that still bring a smile to my face. There was something magical about the thrill of the game, the camaraderie with my teammates, and the joy of competing at a high level. Traveling for games was always an adventure—arriving at bustling airports, feeling the palpable excitement in the air, and dreaming of all the new destinations waiting to be explored. I adored those moments of takeoff, the airplane lifting off the ground, and the world below becoming a patchwork of fields and cities. Each trip was not just about softball; it was a chance to build connections that I hoped would last long after graduation. I remember collecting business cards from fellow travelers and industry professionals, imagining the vast network I would have at my fingertips one day.

Every aspect of that experience resonated with me. I cherished our study hall sessions, where other dedicated athletes surrounded us, each pushing one another to excel—true "iron sharpening iron." Many mornings began long before dawn as we met at the weight room, the faint glow of sunlight barely breaking through the horizon as we worked to build strength together. The shared sweat, the laughter, and even the competitive banter made those early workouts some of the best memories I hold dear.

Many days, I would go in and run for miles and miles on the treadmill. I tried so hard to get the chiseled body that so many female athletes seemed to have as a default. I didn't know it at the time, but I had a thyroid problem, likely given to me to ensure a weight problem, or maybe not. I do know I had the symptoms of it as a small child. I know that it was not diagnosed until it was time for me to start bearing NFL masonic offspring. Suffer until we need you to produce for us. We make you healthy, then send you back to misery once we are done with you. That, in my mind, is the NFL way. Women are objects to be used, then tossed aside.

The summer of 1995 felt blissfully lazy, the kind of season that stretches out like a cat in the sun. I was nestled in the cozy confines of my college rental, the faint hum of cicadas outside my window lulling me into a deep sleep. Suddenly, the shrill ring of the phone shattered the stillness, pulling me abruptly from the realm of dreams. I fumbled for the receiver, my mind still hazy, when a familiar voice crackled through — it was Matt Russell.

Back in high school, Matt had been a force of nature, full of charisma and dreams, but after graduation, he vanished like a mirage, leaving behind unanswered questions and a heart that ached with unspoken words. Hearing his voice again sent a jolt through me, igniting long-buried feelings. He was passing through town and wanted to see me, claiming he had something important to discuss. His invitation was laden with nostalgia, stirring memories of laughter and shared secrets.

He suggested we meet at the Holiday Inn Express, a modest place where teams often stayed when they played the mighty Mizzou. The choice struck me as bittersweet, for it held echoes of youthful aspirations and fleeting moments. I felt a rush of excitement intertwined with caution as I agreed — a part of me was unsure about reopening that chapter of my life, but the allure of reunion was too strong.

When I arrived at the hotel, the air was thick with anticipation. There he stood, taller than I remembered, with an easy smile that brought back a flood of memories. We embraced, and that initial connection felt almost magical — a warmth that reached deep into the essence of who we were.

As we met near the fountain that was inside the hotel, we began to converse. The conversation flowed effortlessly as if no time had passed.

Throughout our conversation, I felt a strange sense of fate weaving itself into our reunion. It wasn't just about two friends reconnecting; there was a cosmic thread pulling us together, and I sensed it in the air around us.

In the whirlwind of emotions, Matt revealed the reason for our reunion — he wanted to get back together and he wanted to marry me. The startling announcement stunned me, pushing me back to the day he ghosted me, leaving my heart fractured. Could it be that this was fate's way of offering a second chance, or was it merely a momentary lapse in a well-planned existence? As I looked into his eyes, filled with sincerity and hope, I knew this was the moment that would redefine our stories forever.

We were back together after seeing each other for the first time since 1993. He asked me to transfer to Colorado and play soccer. I told him that I wasn't good at soccer. As I have often thought about how much better life could have been because I know that he would not have knowingly destroyed my life, I would never wish that my children were not born. It is very difficult to live without your children. It is emotional. It is painful every day. Every day, I open my eyes to reality, and I want to smash them shut and hope that my everyday life isn't the nightmare that I wake up to. In an attempt to paint a woman as crazy, they get her to react in public and make her cry. It's not really hard to do by psychopaths who feel no pain or remorse. There should be a children's book titled "Psychopaths Don't Cry." They don't. They cause people to cry and then make fun of them for crying.

In the NFL's mind they aren't living in reality. They are heroes in their mind for sacrificing my family and wrapping it in dynamite. See, well, sure, we blew up Dawn's family, but it was to save you all…see we are heroes. See, we will paint stuff on the sideline like we are heroes and rah-rah you into joining our team knowing it is one-way loyalty and you are paying us to destroy me and their families…but oh, don't look over there at the Chris Brymer story look over here at our million-dollar equipment that could help feed the homeless but we use it to help guys beat up other guys, better. Whew, it is so tiring to be American Heroes and destroy women and children.

Can we donate to a battered women's shelter to make America forget we help cause a ton of domestic violence calls from brain injuries from former Pop Warner, high school, college, or NFL players? All of a sudden, you try to be logical and reasonable as a man is trying to destroy your life, then wallop. See, look over here.. oh, our million-dollar facilities, our billion-dollar stadium, did we mention we help sick kids? Oh, Chris Brymer's son and his son's stolen childhood?? We don't want to talk about him nor, the boy choked out while in utero. Collateral damage does not get talked about over here at NFL Headquarters. Collateral damage gets tossed in the trash at NFL headquarters after being destabilized.

As a child, I dreamed of becoming a lawyer, inspired by a deep desire to seek justice for those who had suffered. I found myself drawn to the stories of true crime, where I witnessed the profound impact that misguided or malevolent actions could have on people's lives. It was heartbreaking to see individuals endure pain, injury, or even loss, and I felt a strong sense of empathy for those affected. I still carry that empathy with me, motivated by a passion to make a difference in the lives of those whose experiences have been marred by the actions of others.

Chapter 05
Finishing College and Being Human Trafficked to the NFL

I was dating Matt Russell in 1995 when I first caught sight of Craig. He was around the Mizzou athlete weight room area. We had just been warned not to talk to football players, so I listened to what my strength coach said. Part of me wonders if that message was solely intended for me, since most of the masons knew Craig was at Mizzou to get me, destroy my life, and get rewarded by the NFL. I had no interest in Craig and gave him a dirty look. Craig would later tell me that he would use his plan B, which was to infiltrate my friend group. One day, my teammate had moved away and called me up to have me track down the photo Craig was supposed to draw of her pitching. Craig had circled her when circling me didn't work. His goal was to get to the NFL and he wasn't going to get there without me.

How did he know that my grandfather was a 33-degree Freemason? Simple. His NFL masonic mentor, a local retired NFL player. Sure, most pro football players lived in St. Louis, but this one was assigned a job, I am certain, by his former NFL owner, and he came through. Big time for the NFL. He let Craig know that there was a girl highly coveted to be human trafficked to the NFL for masonic lineage.

The NFL mentor also told him other things, like about how the NFL billionaire elite runs the police, and ther first responders through the secret society called Freemasonry. He went and confirmed that through his neighbor and Police masonic mentor, a man we will call TJ Collins. TJ ran St. Clair County Jail in Belleville, IL. Craig asked TJ if it was true. It sure was. It was accurate that NFL elite billionaires ran the state governments and police. They told the police what to do. TJ then taught Craig how to recognize hidden symbolism on police uniforms and by counting the points on badges to know that the elite ran this police force. He also said that they have a secret handshake.

So, let's consider a hypothetical. Let's say that a billionaire NFL owner knocks up a young, pretty woman behind his wife's back, and he doesn't need the public scrutiny or the costly divorce that will likely come when his wife finds out. If he cannot buy the mistress off or get her to go away, he will enlist the police as his henchmen/women to terrorize and harass her until she breaks. That breakdown will discredit her and make her fearful away from the powerful man. That is the Destabilization Program. Did the policeman or woman have a choice? No, not at all. Had that policeman, or policewoman, not followed through with orders to harass an innocent woman on behalf of the NFL billionaire, all of a sudden, the police officer would have been put through The

Destabilization Program. They would find that all of a sudden, they were making mistakes, planted mistakes, at work. They would all of a sudden be getting their children turned against them at school by teachers and coaches. See, the NFL elite billionaires run our state governments. Anyone licensed to work in that state needs their license renewed, and it is easy to control someone through their jobs. It is also easy to control owners of businesses using their license or their compliance with the state as blackmail. That is, in a nutshell, how the elite NFL billionaires run our government through a secret society that every founding father was a member of, the Freemasons. If you follow President Donald Trump's talk, you will hear him reference the Swamp, the Deep State, or the Cabal. What he is talking about is the Freemasons.

While dating Craig for three years at Mizzou, I had anomalies take place. One day, I got off the shuttle bus at Mizzou and saw a girl whom I recognized as working with the football team. She would walk behind me, talking about me to her friend, calling me derogatory names. I have heard she was trying to do that to elicit a public reaction out of me to make me look crazy. I would have a lot of money if I had a dollar for every time someone came up to me and said something rude, looking for that public reaction. I remind you that this is the exact same thing I witnessed my father endure whenever he went out in public. He was essentially a targeted individual.

Also, during Craig's senior season, he created a masonic logo to submit to the Mizzou Athletic Director. It was an upside-down triangle with a tiger in the middle. Craig didn't just say it was rejected. He said that the Athletic Director admonished him for the upside-down triangle. Craig had explained to me the significance of that pyramid for the elite.

The pyramid has a pointy top. The point is very small but is above the wider part. It means there are few elites that run the masses. By Craig flipping the triangle upside down, he had put the elite on the bottom and the people on top. The athletic director did not like that one bit.

Craig thought that by being with the power that Lindbergh gifted me, of the shadow government. He was told he would get a one-way ticket to the NFL if he proposed to me. That is why he would propose to me the night before the 1999 draft started. He got down on one knee in the Mizzou squad. I already knew he was proposing, as he told a friend and she told me. But I gave him the disclaimer that I am sometimes mean. I am Type A. I get in Type A mode, where I am trying to accomplish something or thinking about something, and can react to that. I asked him if he was sure he wanted to marry me. Yes, he proclaimed! He didn't care about disclaimers. All he cared about was that in about 48 hours, his ticket to the National Football League would be punched. Proposing wasn't done out of love. It was done out of necessity. He knew that in me, he had seized my 33 degree33-degree decision-making power that Lindbergh gifted me with the shadow government. He was told he would get a one-way ticket to the NFL if he proposed to me. That is why he would propose to me the night before the 1999 draft started. He got down on one knee in the Mizzou squad. I already knew he was proposing, as he told a friend and she told me. But I gave him the disclaimer that I am sometimes mean. I am Type A. I get in Type A mode, where I am trying to accomplish something or thinking about something, and can react to that. I asked him if he was sure he wanted to marry me. Yes, he proclaimed! He didn't care about disclaimers. All he cared about was that in about 48 hours, his ticket to the National Football League would be punched. Proposing wasn't done out of love. It was done out of necessity. He knew that in me, he was getting his one-way ticket to the NFL.

Before he would propose, though, during the course of dating over my Junior and Senior years, he would take me back to his hometown, which was not far from where I grew up, and to the top of the local county Jail to visit his masonic mentor TJ Collins, who was a former military police and then Superintendent of St. Clair County Jail. TJ would hand Craig the ways he wanted me to look bad, the list of how to win The Chosen One. Then, over 27 years, I was perplexed by the man who said he loved God and would follow the bible but not follow the bible. He would gaslight me, triangulate me with my own family, and master-manipulate me. Once, I ran across an article about dark psychology and gaslighting, and it was like it was written about Craig. I realized that he was learning that from TJ.

I imagine that behind closed doors, TJ, Craig, and the NFL likely had quite the toast, and celebration, this past year. They would know what I did not. Their main goal, together, was to mis-document me and destroy my life. They have succeeded. They deserve a seat in Satan's Hall of Fame. They have a good person suffering every single day when she opens her eyes and does not see her children there. I suffer every single day when I go out into the world and see moms enjoying their children as if it is the most normal and American thing to do in the world. When I hear another child call out the name "mom" or "momma" it feels like I am being shot in the soul, repeatedly.

It is truly frightening when you learn that a secret society is run primarily by men where many played football, which damages frontal lobes in certain positions more than others, and the havoc that can ensue. Football and Freemasonry go together like peanut butter and jelly. It is why every football coach I was growing up around is ready to jump in and discredit me behind closed doors in Masonic Meetings. Dawn or the NFL? If they have low self-esteem, they automatically default to the NFL. It brings them self-esteem to do a favor or attach themselves to the seductive mistress called the NFL. Add on top of it that the man likely damaged the logic and reasoning center of his brain and you have quite a quagmire in the United States.

Chapter 06
Packers, the President, and Secret Masonic Handshake

My ex-husband was drafted to the Green Bay Packers April 19, 1999. The team sent us a box of Packer gear, including some for me. Truly a first-class organization. It is the only franchise owned by the fans. We arrived, and the NFL itself was something to witness. Let me remind you the NFL is the elite. The Packers are a team in the NFL but I don't see each team as aligning themselves with the values of the NFL.

Once we arrived in Green Bay, seeing the NFL for the first time up close, I saw the seven deadly sins on steroids. The NFL is exactly what you imagine it to be and more. One of the first housewarming parties that I attended at the home of one of my then-husband's Packers teammates had two married players show up with their girlfriends. Also, Craig came home telling the story of how one of the coaches was joking about how he ordered hookers with a credit card, and when his wife saw the charges, she wanted to know what it was for "patio furniture," he said. He joked how he immediately had to go out and buy her new patio furniture.

I felt further away from God near all the money and fame. For the love of money is the root of all evil. Money is not evil. Money is a powerful tool that can make a difference. It is the love of that money that causes pain. People will lie, cheat, steal, murder, and exploit to get that money that I won't do. The NFL will, though. It is a business that openly objectifies women. The pressure to look perfect is insane. The NFL mystique is so grossly alluring that now beautiful women line up hoping to grab a spot in the NFL circus, even if it means breaking up a marriage and a family. Truly sick.. If you want to see how fast your girlfriends will flirt with your husband, have him get drafted into the NFL. It changes people overnight, including all the people around it.

Truckloads of money were up for grabs in the NFL. Competition was fierce. It created tension and jealousy. The people of Green Bay were kind, friendly, and warm. They took you in and treated you like family. Green Bay is not a huge metropolitan area like Chicago, New York, or Los Angeles. It is a down-home, down-to-earth place where life is about God, family, and the Green Bay Packers.

In the fall of 2000, President-Elect George W. Bush was to visit Green Bay to visit the practice on Clark Hinkle Field. My husband had been warned in advance. My coworker, who was also married to a Packer player, made plans to attend it. I don't know why I didn't make plans to attend, but I wish I would have. My husband would describe to me the exciting visit of meeting a President-Elect. He said that President Bush was nice. He said that Bush did the Freemason handshake, and when my husband tried to pull away to allow him to move on to the next player, President Bush kept a tight grasp on his hand and said, "Son, where are you from?"

"Belleville, Il, sir," Craig replied.

Craig said that President Bush acted like he knew where Belleville was. Bush continued on down the line shaking hands with the rest of the team that wanted to.

When divorcing, I went to find these photos online, and I had to screenshot and chuckle inside at what I would find. The NFL had changed the Packers' website. Specifically, they changed President Bush's visit to June 2000, which happened to coincide with when my husband was in NFL Europe. They did not, however, remember to change the clothing of turtlenecks and long sleeve shirts that obviously would not be being worn in the middle of June in Green Bay. What caused the date change? Simple. Freemasons are hiding the facts.

In the past few years, the world watched Brett Favre be the center of a welfare scandal that crippled his reputation and his finances. I would view it as Brett being entrapped by the masonic NFL hand that fed him. He was made wealthy off the NFL Freemasons. When Brett began speaking out about CTE, I knew it was a matter of time before the NFL Freemasons walloped his life.

Brett has made the State of Mississippi millions and brought so much notoriety. Several huge stars ask for favors in return for what they have done for their state. I fully, 100 percent believe that Brett had a legal trap set for him to entangle by the NFL Freemason up the river into the entire Welfare Fraud Scandal. Brett had asked for money to build a volleyball facility at his alma mater. The money would be supplied through welfare funds. I would have immediately thought that the State (which is run by NFL billionaires, according to my former NFL player ex-husband) was trying to entrap Brett by going down that route. It turns out that that was exactly what they did, in my opinion.

Thinking back to Green Bay, I remember Craig and I drove around a lot to entertain ourselves. While getting ice cream one day at Dairy Queen, we happened to pull in behind Brett Favre and his wife, who was driving her beautiful gold Lexus. From our view, right behind them in line, we could see Brett recline his seat and put his hat over his face. It was an eye-opener that fame changes everything, including a quick run for ice cream. I imagine that several times over the course of our 2 seasons there, I pondered what it would be like to be that famous. Fame is like a bright light. Useful to stay on track, but sometimes, when too much, it can be quite blinding.

I did not get to know them really well, but anytime I was around Brett or Deanna Favre, they were kind, humble, and down to earth. Oddly, the most interactions I had with Deanna were near the end of our stay in Green Bay. I did an obstacle course with her to promote fitness among young girls. We would climb telephone poles and push a car together. Deanna had been a softball player, and her athleticism showed. It was a really fun time. I would have loved to have continued doing fun things like that as a part of the Packer Wives Association, but Green Bay would be a short stint but actually would be the longest stop of them all.

The money you would see going around was just insane. Fancy, expensive cars all over. Jewelry. The houses of fellow teammates were as gorgeous as one would imagine. I remember Craig's teammate got fined an exorbitant amount of money, and he said, "There goes Christmas," yet he drove a Dodge

Viper worth over $ 100,000. Even though these men were making a lot of money, they didn't like losing any of it.

I grew up so poor and was so intent on never being poor again that I continued shopping at Goodwill, Salvation Army, Yard Sales, and St. Vincent DePaul. I bought a clearance wedding dress for $100 dollars in Green Bay. That was 25 years ago. Now, I write my story from a mattress that I sleep on in my parent's basement. I was human trafficked to the NFL along with many, many women. The NFL wanted to stack the NFL masonic all-star team, so women, without their consent or knowledge, were bartered to players by being given no other options and the illusion of grandeur and riches. I joked to myself today —as I walked my food delivery items to a customer—- that I am on the NFL wife retirement plan.

Charity is huge on teams. Wives of players give time and time and time. Money and time. What does the NFL give them directly? Nothing. When I divorced the former NFL player, the NFL was paying my husband 10, 000 per month. I was left with no home, no money, no kids, no life. The NFL sponsored the destruction of my life, but pats themselves on the back, calling it charity. Knowing the NFL from the inside out? It does not shock me.

I loved football. I no longer love football. It is unconscionable that a product is sold off the backs of men's brains, marriages, and childhoods. I have seen how it's made. It changes you. Every single cell in my body is changed. My ability to swallow food properly has changed (from being choked by an NFL player).

When I zoom out and think of how many blue-collar hard-working Americans work hard to enjoy an outing with their family and what they sacrifice to do it, knowing that people at the top like all loyal viewers "Hoosiers," I struggle and remind myself not to hate. When you hate it gives the hated power over you. I have seen childhoods and marriages consumed,. NFL viewers are feeding the masonic system that enslaves all of us. I have heard Roger Goodell speak of the importance of protecting the shield. I never hear him talk about protecting childhoods, therefore I dub the NFL Satan's Shield. That shield means nothing if one single child has their childhood stolen like my three children have from a well presenting, walking brain injury.

Recently, I learned that Jerry Jones apparently bankrolled my former boss. The Cowboys owner, hired people to ensure that after my divorce, I would be guided to an NFL player. My friend Laura told me that "I was supposed never to know" that I was the granddaughter of a 33-degree mason. These powerful, rich, predominantly white men see us women as cattle. Unbeknownst to me, I was born with an invisible tattoo stamped "Property of the NFL." The same goes for my kids. I had once entertained going to law school and being a lawyer. Craig talked me out of that. Now I know why. I would have been taking my power from under the NFL's control. I was human trafficked to the National Football League, AND AFTER THEIR PLAYER DESTROYED MY LIFE, THEY STILL WANTED TO CONTROL ME. Jerry Jones spent a lot of money to try and ensure that I was sent to John Elway, I am told, but Elway took a handsome payoff to stay quiet about what he knew about my life. Many who lined up to be able to give me their umbrella of protection have accepted money to stay quiet about what they knew about me being Lindbergh's chosen one and to not marry me.

If you go to google and type in John Elway and 33-degree freemasons, you will see an article that he is a 33-degree level of freemasonry. He is the highest level one can attain, and likely ran the State Of Colorado for years. I suspect that my father thought that Elway would show up to help protect me and my kids but Elway took the money to enrich himself. He voted for me in masonic meetings then against me. Back and forth.

I have to explain something very important. My children have been cut out of my life. My former Mother In Law's side of the family is discredited on paper in my divorce due to an uncle that went to prison and having sex offender status looks bad on her side from taking my children. I 100 percent believe her brother was framed for this very purpose. In my opinion? Those who accepted payoffs and are now treated well because the people are on top running things might need to understand that my 11-year-old son who is nonverbal, is the target of those who want the elite on top. Should he go into custody of someone tied to the elitists, it will be back to the elite billionaires on top. You help save me, you help save my son, you likely might be helping save yourself.

I cannot fathom how this has not been exposed other than to say that the pyramid scam called NFL Freemasonry thrives in secrecy. I just celebrated my 3rd Christmas without my kids all sponsored by the National Football League. I am living a mom's worst nightmare where the NFL and the State that they used to help pull off the heist of my children seem to keep tabs on me daily on what I wear, how much I work, and how clean my car is or isn't. I cannot seem to get a decent-paying job. The only job I was guided to had Jerry Jones fronting the money behind it. Pay her enough but not too much to allow her to fight for her kids or get out of her parent's basement. We need her to rely on a man and be enamored with the NFL player we send for her.

As I said, at my former job, my co-worker Anita Arnold turned to me one day and asked me if I had ever thought I was related to Charles Lindbergh. As a matter of fact, I had. Days before I had been at the Missouri History Museum exhibit on the top floor. I have been there many times with my kids but that meant I was busy corralling kids. This day, however, I took my time. I stopped and looked at the photo of Lindbergh and felt like I was looking at a photo of my father.

My co-worker at the job that Jerry Jones was supposedly fronting the money on also asked me if I had named my daughter Brooke, after Brooke's field. No, I didn't know what Brooke's field was. She told me about an airbase where Lindbergh had been stationed in the Army. I researched it, and sure enough, Lindbergh did his Army training at Brook's Field in San Antonio, Texas.

I put photos of myself and Lindbergh side by side, as well as my dad and Lindbergh. I don't need a DNA test but I know that my job did one.

I am perplexed why my life has not changed since this conversation.

In America.

2025.

Image-based business ensuring that NFL strings puppeteer me.

Nothing I do will hide the greed of the NFL and of their fellow pyramid scammers. When I recently saw an article about children in shipping containers who were pumped full of birth control pills so that they could be raped repeatedly, I knew the process that allows the theft of a childhood to become commonplace. My children and I were not put in shipping containers, but make no mistake, we were in a shipping container with NFL stamped on the side.

The main motivating factor is greed. Goodell will repeat how his goal is protecting the shield (meaning the NFL shield). I will repeat that I call it Satan's Shield. He doesn't say anything about protecting childhoods, women, and children. Goodell doesn't say a word about protecting police from when a football player who had one too many blows to the logic and reasoning part of the brain becomes combative with a police officer. Greedy people only think of their bottom line. I was told that my 33-degree grandfather wanted to shut the NFL completely down. I can totally see him thinking that— if he was anything like me. I zoom out and feel like a game destroyed my family. Family and childhood are supposed to be a given in the greatest country on Planet Earth.

The NFL, from what I have read, was a CIA-backed experiment to brain-injure the strong males of American society. I know many men who have been brain-injured by football. If my grandfather had that inside knowledge, I think he knew that to destroy anything effectively, you infiltrate it from the inside out. I think the fact that no other league comes close to the NFL shows that they have, in effect, a monopoly, which is illegal in any other business. Proof that the NFL is out of control. Up until a few years ago, they were tax-exempt. They should be sued and forced to repay American taxpayers for that. The NFL got rich selling brains and childhoods in America.

I repeat.

The NFL got rich selling brains and childhoods.

Mind-blowing, isn't it?

I miss my kids every day. I have been traumatized every day when I open my eyes for 3 years. No ending in sight.

Back to Craig's NFL career. Craig was on the practice squad for the Packers for the 2000 season. December 2000, he would get a phone call from three teams to activate him to their active roster: the Dallas Cowboys, the Denver Broncos, and the Cincinnati Bengals. He would join the Bengals. I would pack up our place in Green Bay and get it all ready for my brother to help me drive our belongings back to Illinois while Craig flew on a dress for the final two games of the 2000 season.

Craig would make it a few months of the offseason with the Bengals and then be released. He would then join the Buffalo Bills.

Chapter 07
The Day the World Stopped Turning

In July 2001, Craig drove to Buffalo to begin his career with the Buffalo Bills and I would join him later during training camp. He made the 53-man roster, and we would begin a new football life in the state that would host the most horrific terrorist attack of all time, September 11, 2001, otherwise known as 9/11.

We would get a small duplex on Big Tree Road in Orchard Park, just minutes from the stadium. We would also attend a team Bible study where we would meet Sammy and Leslie Morris. Leslie was a wife whom I would reconnect with after football was over based on common interests, including politics. She was well-informed about the secrets of freemasonry and believed it had a negative impact on society. In her view, the owners of the NFL were at the top of this structure. I appreciate her perspective, and I wouldn't blame her if she felt she had to choose between protecting her family and betraying me.

What fell on us hard was something I can't believe I didn't see coming. The NFL Freemasons were spying on us in our homes prior to 9-11. The Patriot Act made legal what they were already doing illegally. They task police, fire, and EMTs with the job. If someone crosses one of the NFL Freemasons then one way that the NFL Freemasons dictate using the public servants to take harassment of one of their targets to a whole new level is by taking the information gained by what someone does in their own home, often by themselves, and then references it near that person, in public. It will immediately make the person seem paranoid because a stranger is standing near them and referencing something that only the targeted individual would know. It is un-American. It is evil. It is business as usual for the National Football League. If you want to delve that deep, be my guest. If you want to leave it at them spying on me, that's fine. They do. My friend told me things that he could not have known otherwise if it were not for his police informants who were tasked with the spying.

Then came September 11, 2001. It was a beautiful Tuesday morning in Western New York, and not a cloud was in the sky. We received a phone call that informed us about the terrorist attacks happening in New York City, which is not far from Buffalo. For many hours, we sat glued to the television, watching the news as planes crashed into the Twin Towers and the confusion unfolded at the Pentagon.

Oddly enough, the then-owner of the Buffalo Bills was a man named Ralph Wilson. If you Google it, you can see that he is a 33-degree Freemason. 33 degrees is the highest level one can attain in the secret society of Freemasonry. A simple Google search will reveal a list of them, including Wilson, Mark Twain, Charles Lindbergh, Ben Franklin, and many more. When you attain 33 degrees and when you have a son, he inherits something special from you right from birth. If you're not aware of this gift, it could leave you and your children feeling vulnerable, like there's a hidden target on your backs. It could be a target for murder, betrayal, gang stalking, and harassment. That is what my brother and I were born with. That is why my dad always worried about kidnappings. My kids, now, too, wear that invisible target. Sadly, some of those who targeted us the worst were in the NFL family. I used the term family very loosely. Namely Clark Hunt.

If you have ever read about the Lindbergh baby, you do not see the hidden story of Freemasonry that I see. Charles Augustus Lindbergh Jr was kidnapped from his bedroom on the second floor of the Lindbergh home in Hopewell, New Jersey, on March 1, 1932. What many don't know is that the secret society called Freemasonry runs America. The day Charles Jr was born he became one of the most powerful leaders of the secret power grid that really runs America. Lindbergh Sr was naturally disliked by the other power brokers because he was trying to keep America out of war and do things that could save the country money.

As I stated earlier in the book, it was reported that Lindbergh Sr had a 95 percent approval rating by the American people. Lindbergh Sr is credited with founding the America First group that began criticizing the entrance into World War II. What Lindbergh Sr. also knew was that the Military Industrial Complex was run by Freemasons who make money off death.

The day that Charles Augustus Lindbergh, Jr was born, there was an invisible target on his back put there by the evil team of Freemasons. The hidden influence of certain groups has affected many kids, and it's one of the main reasons I believe we should shed light on freemasonry and consider putting an end to it. What about the idea that there are good Freemasons? They think of money first and not of innocent kids. There is no money to expose it? Funny how evil never asks if it is in the budget to maim innocent soldiers and send them home in flag-draped coffins.

In the aftermath of the terrorist attacks, Buffalo, New York, faced numerous challenges. During this time, Ralph Wilson, the owner of the Buffalo Bills, received notable attention in newspaper reports, highlighting his contributions to the community and the resilience of the city. News reports would say Wilson witnessed the plane go into the Pentagon. As most of us know, a plane of that size would have destroyed more than just the section shown by The Pentagon in news reports. The evil team of Freemasons planned and plotted the 9/11 attacks to continue to do several things. The first of those things included killing and maiming innocent people. The second on the list was to usher in legal spying and doing things that they were doing illegally prior to passing the Patriot Act. The third thing included terrorizing the American public. Get the American public behind a war that would enrich many at the top of the pyramid scheme called Freemasonry.

Anyone who studies the brain knows that when a human being is fearful, they operate with a lower IQ than normal. The evil team of Freemasons wants the American public traumatized because when people are terrorized, sometimes they don't fight back like they should. I believe that a group known as Operation Chaos had a plan aimed at creating disorder in our country. Their goal seemed to be to throw everything into chaos. Their goal was and *is* for everyone to live paycheck to paycheck and in fear. They only want themselves and their evil friends to be rich.

I was so sad and cried for a long time about 9/11. When I could not cry anymore, I would drive to the local mall. I recall going to the mall in Buffalo and seeing a man crying in a suit at the food court. The patrons of the mall all had the same sad face of disbelief over the fact that our country was under attack.

Ralph Wilson, the Bills owner, demanded that every player donate something to the American Red Cross. I have been told by those who witness Masonic meetings that Ralph Wilson is on the team of good Freemasons. I hope that is true. I met him at the Christmas Party and hate to think that I met a mass murderer that day. I do believe he was on the good team.

Craig's contract would not be renewed; therefore, we came home to our offseason home and waited. Craig got an offer to go to the Houston Texans.

Chapter 08
Not for Long

Houston would be the last NFL stop for Craig. After sustaining an unfortunate shoulder injury during training camp, he would be released before the Regular Season. The veterans would joke that the NFL meant "Not For Long," and I remember vivid moments of us perusing injury lists and all that in the days after being cut, hoping someone would pick him up off waivers. But that day never came. I realize that we left the NFL with PTSD. It does a number on your brain—the stress, the high stakes, the constant pressure to perform. Craig walked away, grossing just around 600k and netting just over 400k, a sum that seemed significant but barely accounted for the emotional and mental toll of the experience.

We had begun talking about what we would do after football. It was a sobering conversation, with dreams and uncertainty intertwining. I had taken the LSAT (Law School Aptitude Test) while Craig was still in the NFL, and I wanted to be a lawyer. That dream burned in me despite the challenges. Craig had asked me to wait, suggesting that I help run the business he wanted to form. I look back now and realize how much that request shaped my path. I know that I would have never been allowed to succeed as a lawyer. My path had already been constrained. The only place I have really been allowed to grow is under the construction company co-owned by Craig. Why do I think that is? There are reasons beyond the surface, reasons rooted in history and secrecy because a woman who is the daughter of a 33-degree freemason is nothing but chattel. If it is an offspring of one of the suitable Freemasons, the ones trying to stop the Merchants of Death who want to lead us to war year after year? The road becomes even more treacherous. Then, any offspring of the good team will have hurdle after hurdle put in front of them. The evil team of Freemasons use our government like it is their own slush fund and their own business. And I became a mere pawn in their larger game.

We formed the company with the State of Illinois in 2003. It was the beginning of something that felt promising, but we had no idea what lay ahead. We began working on a business that would last roughly 10 years and gross 3.2 million dollars. I worked very hard. Relentless dedication defined those years. I did a lot of the day-to-day business operations. I drove a skid loader, I helped stand up walls, I met with clients, I did home and garden shows, and day by day, I poured every ounce of energy into that company. I walked away from the marriage to the NFL Freemason with zero dollars and a staggering negative over 100k dollars in credit card debt. The injustice of it all was glaring. See, the NFL owner Freemasons? They also control the court system, including the divorce lawyers. The grip of their influence was felt at every turn. In my case, the NFL did not try really hard to hide the close friendship that was formed between Clark Hunt and Missouri Governor Mike Parson, the Governor who just so happened to appoint the sitting judge in my divorce. It was a display of arrogance, a system rigged in plain sight. Arrogance doesn't try to hide much. It so happened that Governor Mike Parson assigned his hand-picked judge to my divorce, and how I think he is guilty of the crime of malfeasance, which is the failure of a public official. Parson proudly wears his masonic ring on official state business.

Why have so many women been left with nothing after an NFL player's brain fails and they level the family? The reasons are complex yet predictable. It's due to the fact that logic, reasoning, impulse control, and the ability to predict the consequences of one's choices reside in the frontal lobes. And when the damage is done there, everything unravels. The NFL owners knew since the 1950s that the players were turning punch drunk. They knew all along. They knew they were beating their wives and bankrupting them. How did they hide it? Simple. They built walls around the truth, one false narrative at a time. At school, they would use teachers and coaches to alienate the kids from mom and act like mom was a gold digger who lost her mind.

The NFL runs the state government, although I want it stopped. The people should be on top. The NFL reach was too far and wide. If the teacher or coach likes their state license renewed, then they have to frame an innocent, abused mom. They had to play along or lose their livelihoods. Meanwhile, the dad is really the one who lost his mind and leveled the family. Many times, she and the children are a target of the NFL and the other evil Freemasons because if she knew she had hidden lineage on the power grid, she would actually be their boss. So, the system kept her in the dark, preventing her from rising to her true potential. In essence, the NFL actually enjoys destroying some of the women they human traffic to their "family." Family, in this case, is a bitter irony. Obviously, I use that term very loosely.

When I zoom out and see the tragedy and the families that have been destroyed by walking brain injuries that were hidden because the NFL owners controlled the top of the pyramid scheme, I can't help but feel a deep sense of outrage. It should be considered one of the greatest crimes against humanity. A crime is still hidden mainly beneath layers of deceit.

Chapter 09
Getting Masonic Heirs for the NFL

Being described as one more shot at football

In 2005, my husband was working out with a worker we employed at our business. The worker remarked on how Craig still "had it," meaning the ability to play football. What that really was turned out to be more than just a comment—it was a signal to guide us to Denver, Colorado. This shift in our lives was about more than just football. Even though we had been married since 1999 and were trying for a family, we could not get pregnant. It wasn't a simple case of bad luck or timing, as I would come to understand later. We could not get pregnant because the Masons around St. Louis were ensuring that I couldn't go through medical treatment. It was all orchestrated from the shadows. Craig called his agent, and his agent got him a tryout with John Elway's Colorado Crush.

Craig did two tryouts with the Head Coach. Soon, we were moving to Denver, which I loved. The city brought a new sense of hope, and with it, I sought medical help. I started seeing a doctor who would help me tremendously. I did not know it at the time, but John Elway, the NFL Hall of Famer—the man with fame and riches beyond his wildest imagination—would cross paths with me. Our meeting was brief and uneventful, He said hello, and then abruptly backed away, leaving me puzzled.

However, those who witness the masonic meetings want to slice it; here is what I know. There's a larger story beneath the surface, one that I was unaware of. Unbeknownst to me, I was human trafficked to the NFL. John Elway has all a man could ever want. He has hero worship, notoriety, riches, adoration— you name it, he has it. So why would Craig escort John to NORAD, the North American Aerospace Defense Command? Simple. It wasn't just football anymore; it was about something far darker. To craft the plan to use me to bear children on behalf of the NFL. I had become part of a scheme that was beyond my control. Use me to obtain NFL Freemason all-stars carrying 132 degrees from me and 132 from my husband. Unbeknownst to me, Elway would allow me to bear children, but the price was unthinkable. He would ensure that I was given the most ongoing, horrific pain that a mother could possibly imagine. The magnitude of this realization haunts me to this day. I have a NOKIA phone with information on it, and it absolutely blows my mind how aware the NFL, John Elway, and Craig were of how bad my life would be destroyed. Their knowledge of the suffering to come was cold and calculated. The NFL used me just like the women in The Handmaid's Tale.

Craig finished in Denver in 2006. He would move on to New Orleans, where I would be nine months pregnant when he was cut by the Benson Family from their football team. Despite my condition, I had to gather our belongings. I would carry our objects down three flights of stairs, my pregnant belly straining under the weight, both physically and emotionally. We would move on to Austin, where he would play the 2007 season, and

I would give birth to my first child. It was a bittersweet moment, filled with joy and a deep undercurrent of dread. I wonder if there was a toast at NFL Headquarters. I can only imagine the silent celebration. They had secured the first 198-degree NFL freemason in my daughter. She was no longer just my child; she was their next link. I was nothing to them but the Handmaid who delivered their link to the top of the pyramid scheme. That truth stung more deeply than I could ever express.

Craig would finish his Arena career in 2008, in Cleveland, Ohio, playing for the Cleveland Gladiators. That final chapter in his football journey felt surreal. It would be his last foray into playing football. The game had taken so much from us already. We went back to building homes, returning to what felt like a semblance of normalcy. I liked the idea of settling into an everyday life, or so I thought. But deep down, I knew things would never indeed be every day again.

Chapter 10
Dr. Daniel Kelly

In 2008, I opened an email from the NFL Players Association asking if the former player suffered from depression and anxiety. Immediately, I felt a surge of recognition; I knew Craig needed to see this email because those were his primary complaints. The timing of that email felt uncanny, as if it were a message meant specifically for us. Craig would be enrolled in an NFL Concussion Study that would go on to look at an estimated 300 NFL players' brains.

We would travel to Santa Monica, California, to St. John's Hospital, where we would meet the remarkable Dr. Daniel Kelly, the man who discovered in 1999 that the pituitary, an endocrine gland located right behind the eyes, when damaged, would be the dipstick for brain trauma. It was a revelation at the time. Dr. Kelly was brought on board to do a concussion study with Dr. Kevin Guskiewicz from the University of North Carolina.

The testing done at St. John's with Dr. Kelly was incredibly thorough and included a neuropsychiatric evaluation. During the two visits, Dr. Kelly explained how the pituitary, nestled safely inside the brain, can only be damaged in one of two ways: by a tumor or trauma. His manner was calm, almost clinical, but the gravity of the situation began to settle in. Once he ruled out any tumors, he gauged the level of damage to Craig's brain from football.

He looked at an estimated 300 brains of NFL players, and at the end of the study, he told my husband, the former NFL offensive lineman, that his pituitary had flatlined. It is essentially a dead zone in terms of function. Dr. Kelly said that Craig had the worst brain out of 300 former players. He explained that Craig's pituitary function was on par with a woman who had gone over a guardrail, rolled to the bottom of a California canyon, and endured a multi-year recovery. The story left me stunned. Her brain injury looked much different from Craig's on the surface, but inside, they were very much the same. It was a chilling comparison that made me realize the extent of Craig's internal damage.

Conveniently, the NFL bought Dr. Kevin Guskiewicz and brought him onto the NFL Head, Neck, and Spine Committee in 2010, just weeks before we were to get the results from Dr. Kelly. The timing felt suspicious, almost as if the NFL was moving chess pieces behind the scenes. I don't think it takes a rocket scientist to know that the NFL immediately asked to see the results of that concussion study that Dr. Guskiewicz did with Dr. Kelly. It was an orchestrated move, typical of organizations trying to control information. Therefore, it is safe to say that in the Spring of 2010, the NFL knew the man I was living with was going to do horrific things to me, and he did. The signs were all there, but the NFL chose to look the other way.

Craig always had depression and anxiety from the day I met him. Dr. Daniel Kelly is a brilliant man. It's hard not to admire his courage, even as he stands in the shadow of a larger force. It's a shame that Kelly is not all over the news and in articles sharing his discoveries, but I think the NFL wanted to keep that little secret to themselves. The truth was too dangerous to be made public. Kelly told me that when he made his discovery in 1999, he published the results in June 2000. One of his first phone calls was to the NFL. I could imagine how that conversation must have gone. That is why you have never heard the name Dr. Daniel Kelly. He should be a household name, but the NFL owns him, in essence. It's as though his groundbreaking work was buried under layers of secrecy and corporate control.

The most important takeaway from Dr. Kelly's work is that the symptoms of a walking brain injury are anxiety, depression, and memory loss. It's almost like walking into a room and forgetting what you came in to get. His words echoed in my mind. When these three symptoms are seen together, the person should be evaluated for a walking brain injury. It was as clear as day, but too many were turning a blind eye.

Chapter 11
Construction Company

We worked hard for 10 years. I worked so very hard that it is extremely painful for me to look back and have nothing to show for it. I poured my soul into that business, only to be discarded by a former NFL player who held all the power cards— with an NFL Freemason Get Out Of Jail Free Card. The same immunity O.J. Simpson had. Then, when the symptoms of the worst brain out of 300 began manifesting, the NFL had their henchmen in place to do their dirty work. I ran our company with precision and dedication. In 10 years, we had zero liens or lawsuits.

How does the NFL turn a victim into a heathen? The system is simple. They use all the people who live in a state and need their licenses renewed. Doctors, lawyers, judges, teachers, coaches, you name it. If you dare to dial the police on one of their NFL players for something as horrifying as beating you, like Nicole Brown Simpson was on the receiving end of, they will ensure that you get a character assassinated in the most public and humiliating way, just as the NFL helped character assassinate Nicole Brown Simpson, the victim. It's an age-old tactic: discredit the victim and protect the brand. Think back to the horrible, vicious things said about her.

I can now look back and see with clarity exactly which teachers were mis-documenting me, why, and for whom. Take, for instance, one principal of our kids' school. He was having his teachers say things to me that were meant to elicit a public reaction. Several of his teachers would flirt with my husband, blatantly. He was aware, due to his local masonic meeting attendance, that I was to be destroyed. He knew his goal was to help elevate the male—my ex-husband—to The Chosen One, essentially placing him on a pedestal, basically a big election where one of the offspring of a 33-degree mason would be chosen to be famous. So, the school principal set me up. He followed through with ensuring that teachers would brainwash my children away from me so that when the day came that the worst brain out of 300 was choking me, he would be there, ready to help tell the Guardian Ad Litem in my divorce how Craig was a model citizen and I was unstable.

See how that works? You hold the license to the person's job or the school they operate or not. And then, you control them. Sometimes, people with nothing will do anything to be affiliated with the National Football League. Like I said, it is the ultimate business for people with low self-esteem. They crave the association, no matter the moral cost. For many people, like the principal, it is part misogyny, part false idol worship. See how that works? You go to church every week for 50 years, but you still walk around ignoring other decent dads at your kids' school to worship the former NFL player. It's a twisted hierarchy. I saw it. My grandfather did an excellent job in giving me a front-row seat to how women and children get treated like second-class citizens by people who can recite the Bible from front to back. Sure, it is morally bankrupt, utterly devoid of justice, and then some.

Chapter 12
The Beginning of the End

In 2011, my ex-husband was constantly complaining of hip pain. A doctor had told him that he had lost a significant amount of length in his leg from having bone-on-bone osteoarthritis. The doctor told him that he needed a hip replacement. That began my husband's quest to look into getting disability from the NFL. A former teammate had told Craig that he had 15 years from his final game in order to apply for NFL Disability. We began reaching out to NFL friends. I began googling the words "NFL Disability." That led me to the website of a lawyer named Kurt Ward. As I zoom out, I fully believe that Kurt Ward was likely on the receiving end of some bad Freemason treatment, and that accounted for his string of bad luck of being paid by former disabled NFL players.

Kurt took a phone call with us in August of 2011. He explained how he only takes on clients that he truly believes are disabled. He said he might have to litigate the claim. He owned www.NFLdisability.com. To make a long story short, my ex-husband signed an agreement for Kurt to represent him. I did not sign the document. My ex-husband signed a document agreeing to pay 20 percent of his NFL disability income for the rest of his life. Months went by before Kurt initiated the disability claim. When he finally did so, my ex-husband was sent to Independent Medical Exams paid for by the NFL. We also had to track down decades of medical records that we then mailed off to the NFL Disability Committee. August 2012 arrived with a letter arriving from FedEx. We opened the letter from the NFL and were overjoyed. My ex-husband had been approved to get NFL Disability.

Craig would begin getting $10,000 per month from the NFL. None of that money was earmarked for me or our children. The NFL ensured it was all his. Handing a guy with faulty logic and reasoning centers of his brain that amount of money after leveling a woman? That is the NFL way. Men are all to them. Women and children are nothing to the NFL. It leads exactly to where I am today, with Craig asking me for financial help while getting $13,000 a month. The amount was in a break-up such that $10,000 came from the NFL and $3,000 from the Federal Government. The NFL disability did come with a bulletproof vest around it called a Spendthrift Provision. What did that mean? It meant no creditor in the United States of America could file a claim and touch a penny of his $10,000 per month. However, now the IRS is garnishing his wages.

Back to being choked. The joy of getting NFL disability did not last long, though, as Paul Scott of the NFL Benefits Office reached out to Craig on to ask him if he indeed hired Kurt Ward as his lawyer. Craig was affirmative. Paul said that Craig was the 3rd disabled player who had been duped by Kurt. He said Kurt hid himself in the entire process and that Craig should not pay him. I thought that was horrible advice after thinking it over. I told Craig that we should call Kurt. Confront him. Consider paying him cash for one year of representation, which would be around $20,000, while we investigate the claims against Ward. Craig chose not to agree. I was very concerned. I could see that this was going to take us down a bad path. I had no idea that it would be what destroyed our marriage, brain-injured our son, and left me penniless—living in my parents' basement. Paul Scott of the NFL benefits office told Craig not to pay Kurt. A Deputy Sheriff served us with a lawsuit on November 4, 2012. It was sickening. Craig had ignored weeks and weeks of phone calls from Kurt, and he had, in turn, sued us. Not just Craig, but he sued me, too. I was being sued for being accused of attempting to commit theft by conversion. Meaning he thought Craig was going to try and funnel money to me and keep it out of Kurt's hands. Kurt needed not to worry. Craig had no intention of giving me any power over him nor any of his $10,000 per month. We spent several months and several thousand dollars getting me thrown off of the lawsuit. It began a tension in our marriage that is still reverberating, and that would have serious consequences for our children. I had perfect credit for decades. I had no credit card debt other than what was paid off monthly the day we were sued. Now I have every card maxed out and most in collections. The Class President is living in her parent's basement after having my life destroyed by the NFL and Missouri Governor Mike Parson.

In January of 2013, Craig went in for the much-needed hip replacement. He would come out and we would be embroiled right back into lawsuit details. It slowly began to unravel our lives and our marriage. My grandmother and family stressed keeping things private. I have kept private, being choked repeatedly to protect myself, hoping the NFL Freemasons would make it right. My son acquired the symptoms of autism in May 2015. I have the photos and documents to prove it. I am not lying when I tell people he is autistic.

What I have kept private is that his own NFL player father brain-injured him while he was still in my uterus, then again at six weeks old. The kicker is the NFL people involved in telling Craig what to do with his own son. Craig Heimburger's brain injured my son when from crushed the amniotic sac. The day I was cut open to get my son out, there was zero fluid around him. Once Craig choked me and crushed me, there began a leak in the sac. What the NFL Freemasons have done to my son is reprehensible. What they have done to all three of my children is criminal.

In April 2013, Craig emailed Paul Scott at the National Football League Benefits Office. Basically, Craig was told by Paul Scott that he was glad that Craig was fighting Kurt. I like Paul. From talking to him, he sounds like a person who tries to help. Did he know I was dealing with a man who would nearly kill me? Likely not. He knows now. He witnessed me being choked in the Masonic meetings. I have no doubt he has regret and sorrow. He knows he is looking at a Greek Tragedy, as does the former MLB baseball player Andy Benes. I love it when a Christian shows themselves to be a true Christian. Truly. If you can recite the bible front to back, but you choose the NFL player over the victim just to stay cool with the guy who snapped at Brett Favre on occasion, then you are the scum of society. *Truly.*

There it was in writing on an NFL email letterhead. The exact backing Craig needed to justify to me to keep fighting a lawsuit that I knew would bankrupt us. A little more than a month later, Craig would try to kill not just me but his own unborn son. Why? That email has a lot to do with it. That letter emboldened Craig to continue the lawsuit instead of hiding our three homes in my name. That letter changed everything.

On a warm June Saturday evening in 2013, I was six months pregnant with my only son, Brody. We began arguing over the lawsuit and the out-of-control fees. He and I were in our master bedroom while my daughters were with my parents. Suddenly, Craig shoved both of his hands into my chest, and I flew backward, airborne, right onto the master bed. Watching Craig do pass protection for many years, I often wondered what that felt like to get punched in the chest by his long, muscular arms. This was what it felt like. It felt like two jumbo sledgehammers slamming into my chest simultaneously. It felt horrific. The fact that I was six months pregnant elevated my horror. How do you justify him doing that to me? How does any good human justify what they witnessed take place in Masonic meetings?

Craig Andre Heimburger, Jr., died that night. I never saw Craig again. His headstone one day should really read that he died in June 2013. Craig lunged on top of me and began choking me to death while also using his 6 feet 3 inches, 320 lb. body to crush my pregnant belly. When he was on top of me with his eyes just inches from my face, I saw a darkness in his eyes. It was something I will never forget. Those were the eyes that had once been the ones that told me that they loved me thousands of times. That guy who loved me was gone, though. The darkness in Craig's eyes is something I will never forget. The anger and the rage, all directed at me and an unborn baby, his own son, no less. My poor son. My poor, innocent son did not have a chance. It is horrific that the man who did that to his own son actually has fans. You should be ashamed of yourself.

While being choked, my eyes began to feel as if they were going to pop out of my head. It was unimaginable that I could survive much longer if I didn't fight back. What started as an internal question of "What is he doing?" quickly escalated to "Oh my God, I am going to die." In desperation, I struck him on both sides of his head until he finally leaned back, releasing his grip. I bolted out the front door, running for my life, and collapsed onto the grass, dialing my brother's number.

Why didn't I call the police? The answer was simple. I would have been calling a county where his close friend worked, and his friend's father was in charge. Does this mean I believed they were immoral? Not at all. However, I am certain that they answer to the NFL human traffickers who have committed terrible acts—murdering, framing, and destabilizing police officers who refused to follow Masonic orders.

I know EMTs, firefighters, and police officers have been forced to carry out the will of corrupt individuals within the NFL. Of all those who have been manipulated, no one has suffered more than the police. Good officers have been killed, framed, and destabilized. They have been used to carry out the dirty work of these powerful figures, especially when it comes to targeting individuals the NFL seeks to destroy. If I can free myself from their grip, it might just help free the police, too.

I am fully aware that some police officers dislike me, and that's fine. After all, creating conflict between me and law enforcement was part of evil's plan. But I have never had any intention of harming anyone, and I refuse to stop fighting back against the forces trying to destroy me.

I don't know what these other women beloved by voters and police have on the NFL, but I know that I have enough to make sure that the Police never answer an NFL billionaire again. What if this isn't exposed? Evil just continues to steal people's lunch money like it is theirs. Once they amass wealth again, then it is on to plan two: reignite the pyramid scheme to run in their favor. Evil is lazy and greedy. Therefore, they have to ensure that someone else is doing all the work on their behalf. They need henchmen and women. Sadly, that is what they have turned many police forces into. I feel terrible for all the reputations of policemen and women who were destroyed working in the OJ Simpson Case.

I dialed my brother that day. Why? Because the police knew exactly who Craig was. They knew he was an NFL Freemason. Had they arrived, Craig would have given the secret handshake that signaled what they already knew, blaming her. *Accuse her of being the aggressor.* This reflects on the billion-dollar cartel at NFL headquarters. My brother arrived a short time later. When I pointed at Craig and told my brother that Craig had choked me, Craig retorted, "No, I didn't." I watched him become a liar from someone who had just been a double attempted murderer.

I feel as if I didn't do justice in describing how horrific it is to be choked. It is so personal. It is so brutally painful to have your airway blocked off. I felt that my son and I were going to die. I credit Brody with saving my life. I don't think I would have fought like hell like I did if not for trying to save the life of my only unborn son. Later, when my boy saw the light of day, I decided I needed to be by his side — every second of the day. So, I quit. I quit selling real estate for Coldwell Banker after being choked to focus on trying to get my son better, and Craig, too, better from his brain damage.

I struggled to write this chapter. I have evaded typing it, and it is as hard as I thought it would be. It should not happen in America. Yet, daily, we are creating homegrown murderers via frontal lobe brain injuries. I began having trouble with the sac around Brody not long after being crushed and choked by the former NFL player named Craig Heimburger. The amniotic fluid was leaking out. When I was cut open at my C Section, water should have gushed out. It didn't. It didn't because his own father compromised the sac that was supposed to be a safe haven for Brody. My son's birth documents show that the amniotic sac was compromised, and it was compromised by former NFL player Craig Heimburger crushing it.

After having my son, I did tell my OBGYN, Dr. Theresa Knight, who I am told did not pass away as news reports shared, but she was taken into witness protection to testify in the masonic meetings about what I had told her. She was very kind, and I do believe the NFL Freemasons targeted her to destroy. Think logically. The NFL brought into the research of Dr. Daniel Kelly in 2009 by hiring Dr. Kevin Guskiewisz. The NFL knew Craig was the worst brain out of 300 in 2009. I have no doubt that they were monitoring us inside our home, and I was told that there was a video of me being choked when I was six months pregnant. Yet, he is still a hero to many. He had free will. He made an educated decision to target me to traffic me to the NFL. He knew all there was in the playbook and used it to cheat.

He used his proximity to me to make me look bad. He is brain injured and easily controlled, meaning evil is jumping up and down to get him in office. He and Joe Biden. So far, they have seemed to have succeeded. The NFL runs on power and money. Those two things are very seductive to weak people and people with low self-esteem. I watched as people ignored their own families just to get closer to an NFL player, hoping that good luck and money would rub off on them. It truly is sick. I am proud that my grandfather, I am told, wanted to shut the NFL down. I think this election has shown it truly has a chokehold on society.

I loved football, but football should not come before God and family. That is exactly what we've done. We have people working blue-collar jobs in factories, then turning their hard-earned paychecks over to the very people keeping us all enslaved and selling out our country to the highest bidder. Football was created as a CIA program to brain injure the strong male and it is so full of smoke and mirrors and diversions that people gleefully line up with excitement to buy the product whose main purpose is to brain injure the strong males of our society. The byproducts of that product are ruined childhoods, failed marriages, abused both physical and mental to women and children, and financial destruction. I repeat the NFL was created by the CIA to allow football to brain injure the strong males of society.

As for me? I see it. I see the NFL's role in destroying our country. I am not the least bit impressed that they call themselves heroes for providing me an umbrella for a few years while letting their evil sobs sicken me, gaslight me, and mis-document me.

To give you an idea of the power the NFL has, consider this. H.L. Hunt was the owner of the Kansas City Chiefs. His grandson, Clark, is now the owner of the team. In a book titled *Devil's Chessboard*, which details the assassination of President John F. Kennedy, it describes a party that took place in Texas. This party was attended by Vice President Lyndon Baines Johnson and all the key players around him. Johnson, a native of Texas, was surrounded by powerful Freemasons at that party, many of whom were involved in oil, gas, and weapons—industries that make a lot of money when our country is at war. War was something JFK was determined to avoid.

Historians have shown that H.L. Hunt was making statements that "the kid" Kennedy wasn't following orders. What does that mean? It means H.L. and his powerful buddies wanted to launder taxpayer money to themselves, and JFK was getting in their way. Many historians agree that H.L. Hunt, the one-time owner of the Kansas City Chiefs, is the real orchestrator behind the murder of the president with the highest approval rating of all time. H.L. Hunt had everything to do with that murder.

His grandson? He had everything to do with the maiming of my son, my family, my finances, my ability to swallow food properly, and, for quite a while, my ability to see a pregnant woman without having an immediate visceral reaction. THE NFL HELPED MURDER THE MOST BELOVED PRESIDENT OF ALL TIME, AS WELL AS BACKING THE NEAR MURDER OF MYSELF AND MY BELOVED SON. How has nothing changed since 1963?

It's easy, really.

The NFL and its hidden network, including the Freemasons, thrive in the shadows, much like harmful bacteria multiplying unseen. They spread in darkness, and it's time to expose them, to shine a light on this debauchery so that it withers and dies.

These people are not like you and me. Clark Hunt's lead security guy, who went by the name Robert Plant, began contacting me after I reached out to Andrew Jo at NFL Headquarters in March 2022. I legally recorded hours of audio of my conversations, both with Andrew Jo and Robert Plant of the Kansas City Chiefs, detailing what I had endured at the hands of a former NFL player.

How did the Chiefs help? They pulled their strings, contacting their buddy, Missouri Governor Mike Parson—one of their own, fully versed in their secret handshakes. Parson ensured his handpicked judge was assigned to my case, and just like that, my kids were taken from me. On September 27, 2023, my daughter's 12th birthday, my three children went to school and never came home. That day, I was metaphorically kicked to my knees.

While I can't prove everything, there's much that I can. The most damning evidence?

- I have 30 years of medical records documenting my ex-husband's injuries that he left behind.

- I have handwritten notes he sent to Social Security, where he admits he no longer feels empathy. I hope Craig ends up babysitting Parsons' grandchildren soon.

- I have audio recordings of Craig admitting to choking me—legally obtained.

- I have emails from NFL lawyer Lisa Friel to the judge, who was, of course, appointed by Governor Parson.

- I have emails from Paul Scott of the NFL Benefits Office, including one where he tells Craig, "I'm so glad you're fighting Kurt Ward."

- I have three hours of legally recorded phone calls between myself and Andrew Jo, detailing everything Craig put me through.

- I have emails, texts, and legally recorded phone calls with Robert Plant from the Chiefs' security team.

Despite all this, justice has been denied to me. My life remains in ruins because of the power these evil individuals wield. By some of them voting for Craig in these NFL masonic meetings, NFL players even gave Craig a thumbs-up for choking his own son. This is where we are as a society, worshipping false idols and condoning their worst actions because of the game they play.

Craig's NFL mentor and his police mentor DB gave him instructions—what was on the list for their most important masonic meeting—and Craig diligently followed them, cheating the system for nearly 30 years, but no one cared. He snapped the ball to Brett Favre. But all of this only highlights how sick our society has become. Craig is celebrated for doing whatever it takes to destroy my life, just to win. You only applaud a man for choking his unborn son if you stand to benefit from it. If you go to church on Sunday, ask God to forgive you—because you need it.

I used to go to church where I knew many are rooting against me. But I'm not there for them—I'm there to worship God. I've attended Catholic churches, Mormon churches, and more, searching for those who truly value women and children.. I am proud to report that I have found it.

Since the day I was born—on July 17, 1976, a date signifying revolution—I've faced constant challenges. Yet here I sit, another day stolen from me as a mother, while Governor Parson gets to enjoy his grandchildren. I wonder if he'll show off his cute little Chiefs tattoo, proudly displaying his worship of the NFL. To me, it's truly sick and evil. I hope Parson rots in jail, and though I'll ask God to forgive me on Sunday, I still believe evil deserves to be behind bars. Men who destroy childhoods and slander women on behalf of the NFL should die in prison.

PUT IN THE EMAIL FROM PAUL SCOTT TELLING CRAIG TO KEEP FIGHTING. PUT A COPY OF THE EMAIL IN THE TEXT OF THE BOOK.

As I write this, my 83-year-old father is enduring his third Christmas without his grandchildren. He's being blackmailed: "Make your daughter famous or lose your grandchildren." I believe my father, who possesses ESP and absorbs the emotions of others, just wants peace, even if it means sacrificing my well-being. The NFL has the power to divide families that were once inseparable. I want to become famous like Lindbergh and fight for the marginalized. I want to work for this country to ensure that such injustices never happen again.

Each day that passes, I grieve what my father was unable to do, and I mourn the fact that men like Governor Parson get to spend the holidays with their grandchildren while my parents suffer. But I also see a purpose in this suffering. It is why I'm sitting here typing these words. People like Parson and his elite friends don't care about the suffering they inflict—they're too busy hobnobbing with their wealthy, powerful buddies, using others for their own gain.

I'm grateful, though. I'm grateful for the values my grandfather instilled in me, even from afar. I'm glad he made me poor, so I could learn to empathize with the poor. And I'm thankful he shared with me the evil plans of those in power: traumatizing society, enslaving people, and injuring strong men.

I'm also glad that my grandfather gave me this job. I've seen enough to make me sick. When I was around the NFL, I felt further from God. Many NFL players will stop voting for me because their egos matter more than my son, who was nearly choked to death in utero, as well as my daughters childhoods.. I am a human litmus test for morality. I was targeted from birth by people with endless bank accounts, the highest-level technology, chemical warfare, and mind techniques designed to ruin lives. They made my family's life hell, but they couldn't get me to sell out and become one of them.

I will never become someone like H.L. Hunt, nor his grandson, who is well aware of my suffering and chooses to punish me for speaking out while rewarding my silence by allowing his people to vote for me. H.L. Hunt's family should be in prison for their role in murdering the most beloved president of all time. The masons performed a coup on our country the day JFK was murdered. If JFK's casket could speak, it would be emblazoned with a Chiefs sticker and covered in NFL logos.

Chapter 13
Opiates, Hawks, and Destruction

My ex-NFL player husband began an opiate addiction in 2008 that would include over 10,000 opiates ingested over an 8-year period. He was doing this with children in the house. The same three children that Mike Parson and the State of Missouri handed to a man with an estimated 16,000 sub-concussive blows to the brain. If Mike Parson didn't wear a masonic ring and have the same get out of jail free card he would be in jail for malfeasance and corruption for his role in my divorce.

During the choking and opiate addiction period, there were times when Craig had more odd behavior that I had never seen. One night he brought my daughter home from a basket-ball game, and he came in the door and saw my son playing with a Jessie (from Toy Story) doll. My son was pulling the doll's hair, and Craig said that my son was trying to indicate fire. He told my daughters to gather all of their valuables because the house was going to burn down. I could not get him to be logical or reasonable about it. I presume because logic and reasoning are in the frontal lobes, and he used his frontal lobes as a battering ram. My oldest daughter told this story to the Guardian Ad Litem in my divorce. Alarming for sure? Of Course. But I am aware that she had to do what the NFL Free-masons wanted her to do.

That night, Craig drove us around for hours, insisting that the house would burn down. It did not, of course. We came home and I remember being just exhausted. It was absolutely exhausting living with a man whose frontal lobes were acting like a wrecking ball, with his own family being the main target. I even texted my mom during the event, telling her what he was doing to us.

There was also another day when he came home and told me that hawks were showing him where to build a drug treatment center. He demanded that I get in and go see. That night, we wound up with our priest because Craig insisted that the priest needed to know about the miracle of the talking hawks. It was the same night that Craig was transported to the hospital. I knew what was transpiring would be whitewashed on behalf of the National Football League Freemasons. The day prior, we had been having similar interactions, and I texted Craig's mom about the off-the-wall things Craig was saying. Once at her home, she demanded that Craig go see his doctor, which we did. The wild ride getting Craig to the doctor's office was horrific. It was truly something out of a nightmare movie. When I think back to my poor son and what he had to witness, if that video of Craig choking me while pregnant, and the video of this car ride were ever seen, I think that moms would consider wrapping their son's frontal lobes with bubble wrap to protect them. I want the NFL to die. I want it to be shut down in honor of my children and the other children whose childhoods were consumed as a byproduct of business at the NFL.

After Craig spent days talking about hawks, he was finally in his doctor's office; the doctor insisted that Craig could not be having a reaction to a medication he hadn't taken for 48 hours. That was on a Friday night in November 2018. Another 24 hours later, we found ourselves at a meeting in our priest's office. The police were called to the priest's office to try and get Craig to agree to go willingly to the hospital. He wouldn't. I walked out of the room to speak to my mother-in-law. She turned to me and said You better get back in there before he talks them out of taking him to the hospital. As I was returning, the police officer stopped me, saying I couldn't go back in as they had just calmed Craig down. The man who was choking me, mentally torturing me, financially bankrupting me from his walking brain injury, and they were scapegoating me on behalf of NFL billionaires. Once again, I immediately realized that the police, EMTs, and doctors would have to whitewash what was happening, all on behalf of the NFL elite freemasons.

A few hours later, Craig was handed paperwork for a medication reaction at the hospital after an EKG and urine test. I was seething, exhausted. Secretly, I had hoped he would stay there forever if possible. I didn't want him to come home. He should have been held on a 5150 hold for the crazy stuff he was saying. But he had his NFL Freemason "get out of a sticky situation" card, which anyone else in his condition would not have had, and would have seen them hospitalized for up to a week. After that night, when Craig was hospitalized for telling the priest that hawks were showing him where to build a drug treatment center, his mother sent me a text saying she thought

Craig had been in psychosis. She asked, "What can we do? Push our way into the psychiatrist's office?"

What she didn't realize was that the NFL player wouldn't be seeing a psychiatrist at all. He had his NFL masonic "get out of being held accountable" card. This is the way the NFL hides walking brain injuries. They scapegoat women and children.

Craig stayed off opiates and a range of other drugs after that weekend. I, on the other hand, began crafting a way out of the marriage with the primary goal of getting my children to safety. It started with putting our house up for sale. Once we sold it in December 2019, we moved into my parents' basement. Craig moved in as well, and despite asking him to leave on several occasions, he refused. By this point, I viewed him as a terrorist. We both knew I couldn't call the police, who were run by the very NFL billionaires responsible for this problem. I had texted his mother, pleading for her to come and get him, but she ignored my cries for help.

In August 2021, I moved to a rental with my 3 children.. Life had obviously gotten harder after separating from him. This was because of a two fold issue. One, I was leaving the NFL masonic umbrella, and then the NFL was going to take the umbrella and impale me with it while walking off with my Masonic All-Star children. I had hoped that I I might finally get to reclaim some semblance of a life but was realistic that I would have to fight just like I am fighting now. However, once I filed for divorce, the oddities began to pile up. Teachers and coaches were directed to turn my own children against me. I attended a high school volleyball game to watch my daughter play, and at one point, the referee blew her whistle and screamed at her. When I looked across the gym, I noticed a man with his camera trained directly on me. Why? The NFL freemasons had seen the detailed restraining order I filed with my divorce, and now it was their turn to create more "evidence."

The man was the father of a student who had graduated years earlier. Why would the NFL freemasons want to provoke a public eruption from me toward the referee? Simple: to justify that I was unstable and use it as grounds to take my children away from me. I love my daughter's school and would have loved to have gone there myself. I can separate the school from the freemasonry.

One night, I went to give my son spray melatonin, but it clogged. When I opened it, I saw blood inside. I immediately took him to the pediatrician. The nurse practitioner told me I had to call the police—or she would. I decided to wait until after I dropped my kids off at school the next day to prevent them from overhearing the conversation. When the police arrived, one of the officers was Ahmad Rasool. The police didn't help me, and I knew that they likely couldn't, based on Craig telling me that NFL billionaires ran the police, and based on Jerry Parins, Green Bay Packer Head of Security, telling me that the Packers had a network of police across the country. What a living nightmare. It does not feel like I was born with civil rights or human rights. It does not feel like I have the right to life, liberty, and the pursuit of happiness, like our country's forefathers stated.

The next day, I was turning left onto a main road in the city where I was living in Missouri. It wasn't a one-way street, but there was a small sign across two lanes of traffic indicating no left turn during set hours, which I didn't notice. After I made the turn, I was soon followed by sirens. When I pulled over, the police officer bent down into my passenger window and said, "Don't I know you from somewhere?" I replied, "Yes, you were just in my living room about the NFL player I'm divorcing." He knew who I was, and I believe he was stationed, waiting for me to target.

One thing I know for sure: Craig tainted our food and drink. It was textbook behavior for someone with a brain injury, something he had been doing for years. Was he being instructed by DB, his masonic handler? Likely. I won the reverse lottery—being married to a man who would blindly follow orders to maim and destroy his own family to save someone else's. Did my family really need to be destroyed? Exposing the NFL freemasons could have saved so many others, yet here we sit, with those in power still manipulated by those with money. Evil never asks if something is in the budget.

I've spoken to other significant others of NFL players, and many were aware that teachers and coaches were alienating their children. It's reprehensible to think that this has likely been happening since the 1950s. I feel gut-wrenching pain for the women and children who have watched their father or husband, the leader of the family, morph into a shell of his former self. The woman before me? I can't describe how horrific it is to watch a decent human being morph into a psychopath. For me, it was compounded by the knowledge that the people responsible for selling his brain were also running the police force. I also know that what the NFL elite freemasons did to me, they've done to many first responders and their families.

I seriously doubt that the Founding Fathers could have foreseen the devastation caused by building this country on a pyramid scheme. I doubt they could have imagined how it would target minorities, women, and children.

During the time I was divorcing my ex-NFL player husband, strange things began happening. I would go to my car in the morning and find that someone had gotten inside—turning the flashers on or rolling down the windows. I also began noticing a difference in my regular prescriptions. I don't hold this against the pharmacy; I know they are following the NFL Freemasons' rules. My appointments were also mysteriously moved. For example, if I had a doctor's appointment scheduled for 1 p.m. and showed up at that time, they'd claim my appointment was actually at 11 a.m. I've been keeping old-school paper planners for 30 years, and I still have all of them. I could likely tell you where I was on a random Tuesday 20 years ago.

Once all of this began getting very intense, I reached out to a college friend named Mark Greenblatt, who is an award-winning investigative journalist who is now teaching journalism. I described what I was being put through. He said you are describing the Destabilization Program. Mark said that he had seen that used on people leaving the White House and Pentagon. Mark said that he had seen the Program used on people who were leaving either place with a story to tell that those in power wanted to discredit to make the person look crazy. I believe that is exactly what I was put into. The NFL elite Freemasons' main goal was to discredit me from the story I was about to talk about being choked six months pregnant and then nine more times, and financially leveled.

Chapter 14
The Weapons Of Masonry

Gaslighting and Dark Psychological Operations

My ex-husband displayed what my counselor described as typical brain-injured behavior. Over time, it became clear that he had been putting substances into the food and drink consumed by me, our kids, and even my parents. I eventually caught him in the act one day while he was grilling burgers for my parents. The realization that he was tampering with our meals was horrifying, but it fit the pattern of his erratic and dangerous behavior.

Not long after, my car began experiencing a persistent fume problem. Given that Craig's family had ties to the car business, he took it upon himself to handle all the vehicle-related issues. For over a year, my children and I unknowingly inhaled toxic gas fumes while Craig pretended to take the car in for repairs. Each time, he backed the car down the driveway, acting as though he was heading to the dealership to fix the issue. However, when I eventually reviewed the invoices from the car dealership, I found that he had never addressed the fume problem. Instead, he focused on unrelated services like oil changes or fixing the airbag—anything but resolving the deadly fumes we were exposed to daily.

For more than a year, three innocent children and I were subjected to the harmful effects of chemicals like MTBE,

Ethylbenzene, and Xylene. These compounds all have one thing in common: they're found in gas fumes. It was a slow and silent poisoning that left us with no option but to endure, unaware of the extent of the damage being done to our bodies. My children were turning pasty white and I was having headaches and my hair was falling out. My daughter was sleeping with ice packs for the headaches she was having from the fumes. Yet, today, she is with the monster who was doing it.

Desperate for answers, I hired a private detective. He and his partner, with over 40 years of combined experience, arrived to investigate the issue. After examining the fume binder, they delivered chilling news: they suspected that Craig had punctured the gas cap in my car, intentionally causing the fume leak. I believed it was likely too. Craig had asked to borrow my car right before I was scheduled to take it in for the fume problem to be repaired. Of course, during that time, he had also made a convenient stop at an AutoZone. Given that one of his family members had close ties with the employees there, I couldn't shake the suspicion that they had helped cover for his actions. It's frightening to think how easily people can conspire to protect someone, even if that person is attempting what I now consider a quadruple murderer. I have no doubt that a major reason why my children were taken from me, on behalf of the NFL freemasons, was to conceal the fact that Craig had been poisoning them, filling their bodies with harmful substances. The toll on my body and my mother's has been severe, but my heart breaks most for my children. My son, who barely weighed 60 pounds, had chemical levels in his system that were at 95% for some of these toxins. His own father choked him while he was still in utero, shoved him off a couch when he was just six weeks old, and later, poisoned him with horrific chemicals. All of this was done by a man who many still regard as a hero simply because he played in the NFL. But to me, he's no hero. True heroes find ways to protect and save their families, not destroy them. He agreed to wrap his own family in dynamite to experience being an NFL player. That was the deal with the devil, and he took it.

My daughter began complaining that her school lunches tasted like medicine, which only added to my growing list of concerns. I have zero doubt that one of the primary reasons a man with the brain of a psychopath now has sole custody of my children is to hide the damage he's caused. The fact that no one seems to be in any rush to correct this atrocity is maddening. The schools were tasked with either fixing their bodies from what he had done or adding stuff to their bodies to frame me further. Whatever the NFL Freemasons ordered is what was carried out, I am sure.

If this situation isn't made right soon, my goal will be to hold the parties involved accountable, making sure they pay a hundred times more than what they thought they could get away with. There is no price you can put on what has been done to me and my children, and the situation is all the more sickening knowing that it was orchestrated under the banner of the NFL—a league that continues to protect its own at the expense of countless innocent lives.

For several years, my children and I would undergo regular hair analysis. Every time, the results would come back with the same alarming conclusion: our adrenal systems were under immense stress. It was as if our bodies were constantly locked in fight-or-flight mode, though at the time, I didn't fully understand the extent of what was causing it. Tonight, as I sit here reflecting on everything we've been through, I am overcome with disbelief. My children will go to sleep under the roof of a man whose brain is, by all accounts, even more damaged than Aaron Hernandez's. This reality gnaws at the very core of my being—it underlies every thought, every breath, every second of my existence. It is the reason I keep pushing forward. Even though I may not display my pain as openly as others, it is very real. They may believe my silence or stoicism means I don't feel the weight of it, but I assure you, it exists. The pain is there, constantly simmering beneath the surface, and as I've said before, it will drive me to ensure that the people responsible for this nightmare pay 100 times more than they ever anticipated—unless this wrong is set right, and soon.

Donald Trump was elected, and now, he is just two weeks away from taking office. The fact that someone like him is ascending to the presidency gives me hope. It makes me feel like people like me will finally be able to exercise our Freedom of Speech without fear of being silenced. And that is why I've decided to write this book. I've been waiting for the right moment to pull the trigger on this story, and that moment has arrived with Trump's imminent leadership. I now know that my life's mission will be defined and dedicated to speaking out about the truth—about the freemasonry ties that have influenced my life, about being choked while pregnant by an NFL player, and about being systematically poisoned and sickened by that same man, along with my innocent children.

Do I think this is my dream job? Absolutely not. This isn't what I envisioned for myself in any way. But here I am, faced with a brutal reality, and I will not back down from telling the truth, even though it's far from the path I wanted to take.

The diehard football fanatics who live and breathe the game—they're blind to what really goes on behind the scenes. They don't care that their beloved sport destroys lives. In fact, they're willing to sacrifice their sons on the altar of the NFL, serving them up for brain damage without a second thought. I have no intention of doing the same. Craig has already inflicted more than enough brain damage on our son to last a lifetime. I used to enjoy watching football. I didn't think it was more important than God or family, but now, it's ruined my family in ways I can hardly describe. How do you reconcile that while being held hostage by the very thing that tore your life apart?

More than anything, I would love to focus my energy on helping those who truly need it—people who are homeless, people suffering from diseases, the vulnerable and forgotten. I want to run for public office. I want to be in rooms where important decisions are being made, and I want to put the NFL out of business. I initially didn't want to talk about the NFL, but here I am, forced into it because of what this league has done to my life. As well, knowing that my grandfather had 100 percent of the information and his opinion is that he wanted the NFL shut down, makes me feel like I want to finish the job for him. I think his morals made him observe what greed was doing to this country, and what the NFL was doing to this country, and he felt a sense of duty. I now feel that sense of duty. The NFL was created to brain-injure strong males. Stop glamorizing an entity created to destroy our men and sons. I want to throw up when I see an NFL field painted with the words "it takes all of us." Nah really it takes you being less of a greedy son of a bitch, that's what it takes. It takes you having morals. Which you don't. I hear Stan Kroenke is voting for Craig to win the Chosen One. My hope is that we can remove his wealth and let him live in my shoes, and then see who he votes for. Let Craig choke him out, and see if he feels the same.

Chapter 15
The Divorce

It was very important to me to make my marriage work. I wanted to get married once and go until my final breath, until that almost came while pregnant in June 2013. I tried all I could to help heal my husband's brain and nothing worked. I was choked 9 more times and thrown into a dresser. So, I filed. I attempted to get him to mediate for 2500 dollars starting in June 2020 s, and that is when my fume problem started. I filed for a divorce in November 2021, hoping that I was taking my power back, but knowing that he was an NFL Freemason and that his NFL owners owned the courts. Things were about to take a serious turn now, not that they weren't already. But here, some more people were going to be a part of this "game" in which my problems only grew, but the level I couldn't clear.

There were two officers I want to talk about here. The fume problem in my car eventually led me to hire two private investigators: Because his life was made a living hell, I'm told, I will use the fictitious name of Robert, a retired 25-year St. City Police detective, and let's call him David, an off-duty St. County policeman. They were both highly experienced and came with solid reputations. They conducted a thorough investigation into the persistent fume issue in my car, one that had plagued me and my kids for over a year. After a detailed inspection, they didn't mince words. Robert and David both concluded that Craig was actively trying to kill me and my children by exposing us to toxic fumes, and they stated their intent to take the evidence to a local prosecutor to discuss potential criminal charges. (The names of the officers have been changed to protect their identities.)

However, not long after delivering their findings, both investigators started acting distant, almost like they were backing away from the situation entirely. It struck me as odd. I later found out through a mutual acquaintance that Robert had abruptly lost his job, which made no sense given his years of dedicated service. Something wasn't adding up. Curious, I decided to dig deeper and Googled David's name. For years, there had been no negative information about him online, but shortly after his involvement in my case, things changed. Suddenly, David was arrested for a DWI, a complete shock to anyone who knew him. I have no doubt in my mind that this sudden downfall was no coincidence. David had rendered his honest opinion about the fume problem in my car, and I believe he was being destabilized for speaking the truth.

I saw David a few months ago, and when I asked him about his work, he simply told me he was "retired" from the St. Louis County Police. Something about his demeanor told me there was more to the story, that perhaps there were forces at play much bigger than we could have anticipated. I began to speculate that David, like so many others, might have been caught up in something larger—perhaps connected to his family background. It wouldn't surprise me if he had a hidden lineage tied to the Freemasons, a legacy hijacked by his employer to manipulate him. My friend told me that David was paid off handsomely by the NFL, months after being told that I googled his name and the former detective had bought a house well over a million dollars. I believe that he did indeed get the NFL payoff, not just to stay quiet. I encourage everyone to expose that they have been paid off.

As if things couldn't get worse, I was assigned to a sitting judge, handpicked by Governor Parson himself, a man known to associate with Clark Hunt, the owner of the Kansas City Chiefs. The ties to the NFL seemed to be closing in around me from every angle, as if the entire system was rigged against me. My lawyer, someone I should have been able to trust, refused to admit crucial evidence that proved I had been choked by Craig. It was as if the very foundation of justice was being chipped away right in front of my eyes. Parson proudly wears a Masonic ring in plain sight.

I remember vividly the day when my 2nd lawyer began threatening me, saying these threats were coming from the Guardian Ad Litem and the judge in my divorce. There absolutely was a rule called 60.61 that the judge violated, ordering me to a psychiatric evaluation with no motion filed by my husband's lawyer asking that I be evaluated. According to Colonel Fletcher Prouty, when you see a deviation from standard operating procedure, there is a conspiracy. They were, in my opinion, attempting to pressure me into silence. But what caught me off guard even more was when my lawyer turned to me, with a look of disbelief and helplessness, and said that in all her years of practicing law, she had never seen another woman treated this way. She whispered that she believed freemasonry had a hand in the injustice I was facing. It made sense – the invisible strings of power and influence seemed to pull all the right levers against me.

To add insult to injury, the NFL itself inserted its power into my case, directly emailing the sitting judge. What was once just a toxic marriage had escalated into something far larger – a battle against the NFL machine, one that had weaponized chemical, legal, and mental warfare against me. It wasn't just what Craig had done to me or what was slipped into my food, drink, and even prescriptions; it was the mental games, the manipulation, the gaslighting. It was like I was fighting an entire empire, and I was all alone.

I left the divorce with absolutely nothing. Craig, on the other hand, walked away with our children and a monthly payout of $13,000, a clear testament to the imbalance of power. He had gone through every penny we ever had, bleeding our accounts dry while the bills piled up – over $200,000 worth. But the worst part wasn't the money. It was the humiliating reality of trying to maintain a shred of normalcy for my children amidst it all.

I'll never forget the time I sat with my child, trying to create a moment of joy as we opened presents together. What should have been a simple act of love and celebration was tainted by the ever-present sense of being watched by a representative of the court. It was suffocating. There was no privacy, no space to heal or even pretend that things were okay. Every smile I tried to muster was weighed down by the heavy knowledge that everything I did was being scrutinized, as if I were the one under suspicion. It was humiliating, degrading, and a constant reminder that this was no longer my life to control.

www.ingramcontent.com/pod-product-compliance
Lightning Source LLC
Chambersburg PA
CBHW051223120626
46547CB00013B/1487